ART OF THE HEART

THE DOCTOR–PATIENT PARTNERSHIP

JAY H. KLEIMAN, MD

ADVANCE PRAISE

"Dr. Kleiman's memoir is a pleasure to read, both warmly personal and highly professional. He has shared the details of some of the most challenging and interesting cases from his many years as an invasive cardiologist. Dr. Kleiman's diagnostic acumen is evident in many of the vignettes as are his technical skills. I was struck by the evidence of advances in cardiology leading to very different treatment of similar conditions encountered years later.

"Shining through is Dr. Kleiman's devotion to his patients and his selfless pursuit of the very best care for each of them. Every new clinician will benefit from his modeling...and many of us older ones can learn from him as well."

– Moreson H. Kaplan, M.D., F.A.C.P.
Associate Clinical Professor of Medicine
Yale University
Medical Director Emeritus
Yale University Health Service

"*Art of the Heart*, by Jay H. Kleiman, MD, is a personal and poetic insight into his life in medicine. Each chapter is a story ("a mystery") with his reflections on medical history, technology, and advances in diagnosis and treatment. However, Dr. Kleiman wrote *Art of the Heart* with a purpose: it is for medical students who need a course in 'doctoring' since their medical training, which emphasizes science and technology, inadequately teaches the 'interpersonal, human side of practice.'

"This book is a satisfying read for nurse practitioners who will recognize its patient-focused emphasis on listening, attending, touching, caring – as well as curing. *Art of the Heart* can also be valuable in the education of nurse practitioners, as they learn to create the human connection essential to providing optimal care that leads to healing. *Art of the Heart* will also fascinate the lay reader, intrigued by the science of medicine, who also wants to understand the frequently frustrating medical experiences that we encounter today."

– Nina Adams, MSN Yale University (retired)
Nurse Practitioner Yale University Health Services
Instructor, Yale School of Nursing

"Some of us remember a time when doctors knew who we were as well as what was wrong with us. As modern medicine continues to focus more and more on specific areas of illness, doctors seem to have moved away from relating to us as total human beings. Dr. Kleiman shares with us how one physician pioneered new ways of treating patients' hearts, while at the same time managing to maintain old ways of treating his patients as complete human beings.

"Share a warm and thoughtful voyage of development and discovery through the eyes of a kind, creative and compassionate human being who is also a skilled and talented physician."

– David M Walton, PhD. Clinical Psychologist

"*Art of the Heart* is a moving recounting of one man's journey through a thirty-five-year medical career in the field of cardiology – from student to experienced practitioner – and the timeless lessons he learned along the way. By sharing significant vignettes from that career, Dr. Kleiman shows that for all the marvelous technological advances in medical science, it is the ancient and fundamental relationship between doctor and patient – human treating human – that leads to healing. This book is a must-read for any aspiring medical student who hopes to make a significant difference in their future patients' lives."

– Roger Rueff, Phd
Screenwriter: *The Big Kahuna*
Playwright: *Hospitality Suite: A Screenplay*
Author: *Discovering the Soul of Your Story*

"Dr. Kleiman's book is a master class in doctoring. It is a must read and a prompt for every doctor, whether they are just starting out or have years of experience. The chemistry of the doctor-patient relationship can be more effective than the chemistry of prescribed medication. After reading Dr. Kleiman's book, you are left with a detailed blueprint that both instructs and encourages the physician reader to develop the interpersonal skills so necessary to today's medical encounters. For the lay reader, he sets a new standard and level of expectations."

– Pamela Frankel, MS Organizational Development, MS Child Development

"Every person would want their doctor to read Dr. Kleiman's comprehensive treatise on the fine art and science of doctoring. Less a critique and more an important reminder, Dr. Kleiman's book beautifully outlines the fact that technology and a genuine doctor-patient partnership can coexist. Patients appreciate feeling 'cared' for. Doctors also benefit from the satisfaction of this bond with patients that can help prevent burnout. This book is a must read for every practitioner."

– Larry Frankel, MBA

"In *Art of the Heart*, Jay Kleiman shows readers how crucial humanity and presence are in the care of patients. His narrative grounds us in his life and in society more broadly, taking us through medical training and practice starting in the 1970s and concluding at the start of the new millennium. He learns to work with others to navigate complex hospital systems with empathy, consideration, curiosity, and kindness. We learn of pivotal advances in cardiology, from the early days of angiography, catheter-based angioplasty, and stents. Jay shares his joy of learning and teaching about the heart, whether with students, colleagues, his patients, his mother, or his son, Brian. He brings wisdom and compassion to stories that have helped animate and define his professional life.

"Trust, compassionate communication, teamwork and judicious use of skills and judgment are the bedrock of Jay's excellence as a physician. He captures the miracle and privilege of being a physician in his writing. He listens to his patients, hearing 'the music beneath the words.' His stories from practice are always informative, often gripping and occasionally dramatic.

"Dr. Kleiman does a great job explaining medical terminology and concepts for lay readers. His narrative serves as a wonderful teaching model for physicians and cardiologists. Jay has learned both the power and the limits of his technical skills, when to push ahead and when to stop, always focusing on his patient's wellbeing, never taking undue risks. These are key skills for all physicians to develop and exercise in their own practices. So, too, is the central importance of communication and connection physicians must have with their patients. As he states, 'we must recognize – and remember – that the human component of medicine and doctoring remains essential to healing.' I am grateful to Jay for helping guide us along this path."

– Joseph D. Stern, MD
Author of *Grief Connects Us: A Neurosurgeon's Lessons on Love, Loss, and Compassion*

Heartfelt Press

Chicago, USA

Copyright © Jay H. Kleiman, 2023

ISBN 979-8-9893218-0-3

All rights reserved. No part of this book may be reproduced in any form without permission in writing from the author. Reviewers may quote brief passages in reviews.

Published 2023

This book is a work of non-fiction and contains true stories presented for medical education purposes and for discussion by lay readers. The names have been changed to protect patient privacy except when in the public domain. No medical advice is given or intended. If you have medical questions consult your physician.

No part of this publication may be reproduced or transmitted in any form or by any means, mechanical or electronic, including photocopying or recording, or by any information storage and retrieval system, or transmitted by email without permission in writing from the author.

Neither the author nor the publisher assumes any responsibility for errors, omissions, or contrary interpretations of the subject matter herein. Any perceived slight of any individual or organization is purely unintentional.

Brand and product names are trademarks or registered trademarks of their respective owners.

Cover design: Jennifer Stimson

Editing: Irene Connelly

Project manager: Madeline Kosten

Author photo courtesy of: Sara Levinson

DEDICATION

To all the patients who trusted me to use skilled hands and a caring heart
To all the physicians who answer the calling

CONTENTS

"Brushstrokes"	xv
Author's Note	xvii
Foreword	xxi

Part I
MEDICAL SCHOOL, 1968–1971

1. Inspirations	3
2. In the Beginning – Learning the Bible	11
3. Ambulance Ride, Jerusalem	29
4. Learning from Experience	37

Part II
INTERNSHIP AND RESIDENCY, 1971–1975

5. Teamwork	47
6. Persuasion	57
7. Medical Mentor	65
8. Politics of New Technologies	73

Part III
CARDIOLOGY FELLOWSHIP, 1975–1977

9. Plaque-Buster Pioneers	89
10. Knot What We Expected	107
11. "My Son, the Doctor!"	115

Part IV
PRIVATE PRACTICE, 1977–1998

12. "Trust, but Verify"	127
13. Based on Trust	139
14. Walking the Tightrope	161
15. Challenges	173
16. Impact of Intervention	181
17. Hourglass Artery	187
18. Benny's Nap	201
19. When in Doubt	209

20.	Timing Is All	223
21.	Hearing the Music	237
22.	Guardian Angel	245
23.	Diane: A Cause for Worry	253
24.	Gathering the Team	259
25.	You Better Be Right	273
26.	Patrick: Power Dynamics	293
27.	A Near Miss	301
28.	Back to Basics	315
29.	Memories	323
30.	Brother Fred	339
	Epilogue	345
	Acknowledgments	351
	About the Author	355
	Thank You	357

"BRUSHSTROKES"

If the memories of clinical journeys from times past,
Are like an impressionistic painting of many brush strokes,
Diverse colors speaking together as if with one voice
Each stroke different yet blending with its neighbors.
If each memory reflects a happening from a time remote
Yet still true and instructive in its recounting,
Each memory opens a door to understanding,
A lens bringing the current puzzle into focus.
Now let your mind put them together to unravel a new clinical challenge.
Let the brush strokes become a picture, however complicated or complex, one that will help answer the current question,
A question at first obscure and shapeless,
But which remained so, only until its pieces took form,
Where before its unrelated colors were not yet a picture.
Then reflect a moment, where have you traveled?

What have you seen and learned from past experiences?
Bonds formed in knowing patients' lives over time,
Experience, perhaps of future relevance not yet recognized.
You were present, a Presence!
Learning in those moments, from watching, listening,
Building a store of knowledge quietly taking hold
A gift of growing experience
Commitment, concern, even if silent
Each case resolved, an affirmation, adding to your abilities.
Stop, pause, look back, for a moment.
See the larger pattern, as if each case was itself a brush stroke,
That gave shape to an even larger picture.
A mural recognized from afar, through time and distance.
The realization again of receiving, even as you gave of yourself.
The satisfaction of having answered a calling,
Entered a vocational realm,
The honor and privilege of saving even one life.
Although helped, but not created by technology.
Formed by spiritual bonds,
An unspoken promise with each interaction.
Two people coming together, a doctor and patient,
A relationship of caring and compassion, trust and respect,
Doctor and patient working as one,
To heal.

– Jay H. Kleiman, MD

AUTHOR'S NOTE

Why begin a book of medical stories with a poem? When I was courting my wife, Georgi, I wrote love poems to her every day. They helped me to express feelings that were deep and intense. This book is my love letter to medicine. Each chapter is complete in itself, focusing on the bond between doctor and patient that is necessary to the healing process – yet all together they illustrate a lifetime in, and love for, the practice of medicine.

The sacred bond formed when a doctor cares for another human with a medical need is what elevates medicine from a profession to a calling. The call is to serve others.

Reflecting on my thirty-five years in practice, I realized that medicine became my spiritual home, a place where I lived my values while mastering the skills that could return patients to health. In my case, the values guiding this relationship were based on the core religious traditions practiced in my family. I learned from these rich traditions at home, through prayer and ritual, but as I went out into the world of medicine, I lived them every day.

Over decades of practice, knowing each patient as an individual with a distinct life story and history often revealed a critical element that helped me understand what was needed for healing to occur. This intimate knowledge provided clues to unraveling diagnostic puzzles. From my very first patient, I learned that the human connection remains essential to providing the optimal medical care that leads to healing.

Much of medical training focuses on science and technology, with little emphasis on the interpersonal, human side of practice. What qualities are fundamental to building the human connection and the physician-patient relationship? Competence, commitment, caring, and compassion. Showing respect for the patient serves to close the initial gap in what can be an unequal relationship. Each of these qualities is as vital to restoring the patient to health as the surgeon's knife or the doctor's medications.

Even as I rode the wave of catheter-based interventional technology in my career, I learned that technology cannot replace good bedside medicine. In the age of high-tech medicine, patients continue to want and need high touch. The addition of a doctoring course to the medical school curriculum places a necessary emphasis on the psychosocial needs of patients and seeks to address these needs. In providing personalized care, both patient and physician benefit. The patient feels cared for and the physician experiences satisfaction in the care delivered. Long term, this prevents physician burnout.

These stories are my gift to medical students, trainees, and young doctors. In sharing them, I hope to help all readers develop an approach to forming and maintaining the human connection vital to healing.

Jay H. Kleiman, MD, FACP, FACC, MPA
Chicago, Illinois
November 1, 2023

FOREWORD

For many years, I felt adrift with my longing to listen to the stories of my patients. In medical school, I was surrounded by giants in my chosen field of Internal Medicine and subsequently Cardiology. While we all were taught the importance of a quality physical exam and careful history, the nuances of how the human narrative shaped both the patient and the physician were just beginning to be explored in the world of what is now called Medical Humanities.

Dr. Kleiman's magnificent book will surely resonate with many of our common generation, but also should be mandatory reading for any aspiring premedical student, medical student, or physician in practice at any age. It is a lovely, kind, gentle exploration of the human spirit and its' ongoing challenges in the constantly changing world of health care. He has a unique gift for not only the storytelling of a singular encounter, but for exploring that into the larger metaphysical world in which we all live and work. Like many master teachers, he is able to see beyond the details of a single patient to flesh out the larger questions, obstacles, hopes, and dreams that we all share with our patients. He quite easily shifts from the personal to the communal aspect of health care delivery ... no small feat in a complicated and often polarized world of health care.

His work is truly a gift, and I intend to share it with my colleagues in the Medical Humanities Program at Baylor University. I believe our young students will be inspired, moved, hopeful, and yes – even humbly frightened – by this hugely significant book. It is shaped by compassion, the art of listening, and genuine human caring for those who sit across the bedside from us day in and day out. His lifelong yearning to listen to these narratives has been a gift not only to his patients, but to those of us to whom he has bequeathed these lovely words.

10/07/2023
Michael Attas, MDiv, MD
Baylor University
Waco, Texas
Author, *Medicine at a Crossroads* and *Fly-Fishing—The Sacred Art*

PART I

MEDICAL SCHOOL, 1968–1971

1

INSPIRATIONS

Through the ages, all cultures and societies have had healers. These healers may have been called medicine men or shamans, but however named, healers played a central role among their people, valued as spiritual leaders with special powers and with stature equal to the chief's. Healing was the foundation for a strong and healthy community.

Today our healers are called doctors, trained in specialties and subspecialties. Medicine has become a profession with a specific knowledge base and skills. It is a vocation, or calling, based on the human bond and implied contract between physician and patient. As such, it creates a sacred trust that adds a spiritual component to the relationship.

As far back as I can remember, I wanted to be a doctor. I don't know if I ever thought seriously about any other career. My father's experiences as a young man clearly influenced me. Dad was first-generation, the only son in a religious Jewish family. Education, hard work, reverence for tradition, and ethics were emphasized. Despite his career aspirations, my father experienced frequent antisemitism. When Dad applied to medical school, he had already been told multiple times that with the influx of Jewish doctors from Europe before World War II, no more Jewish doctors were needed. He became a chemist. This field was a second choice that benefited from his creativity and curiosity – he worked on treatments for malaria, which let him contribute to the collective effort that ultimately saved thousands of lives. The practice of medicine was a goal he never reached, and it was expected that I would do so in his stead. After completing a bachelor of science degree, I applied, and was admitted to, medical school. I felt very proud that I had achieved a goal that eluded Dad.

My earliest memories of a doctor-healer are of being ill with a sore throat. The doctor arrived at our house wearing a long black overcoat and carrying a small black bag in his right hand. Spectacles hung off the end of his nose. He spoke quietly to Mother for several minutes. Then, before coming into the bedroom, he paused and washed his hands with warm water.

"It's cold out there and I don't want to chill you," he said as he turned toward me.

He asked me several questions about how I was feeling and how long my throat had been sore. I felt very grown-up, being addressed directly by this important and imposing man. I tried very hard to answer his questions, but it was painful to talk.

He began to examine me. He felt the side of my neck at the back of my jaw. "Your glands are swollen," he said. Next, he looked at my throat with a tongue blade and small flashlight, and finally, using a special tool, he examined my ears. Then, he took his stethoscope from his pocket and warmed it in his hands. He put it on my back and moved it from side to side as he asked me to breathe deeply. When he finished examining me, he again turned to my mother and asked, "Has he had an elevated temperature?"

"It has been 101 degrees for two days."

"His throat is inflamed, and it looks like he'll be needing some penicillin." With that, he took a prescription pad from his black bag and wrote for the medication.

I never thought of it until many years later when I was in medical school, but from a traditional perspective, my doctor's visit followed established medical protocol and had been complete: there was a dialogue involving my mother and me to take my medical history; a hands-on physical examination; and finally, a synthesis of his observations that resulted in a differential diagnosis and a prescribed treatment plan.

Early wooden stethoscope for listening to
patient's heart and lungs

Over the past fifty years, remarkable tools and technologies have been developed for delivering medical care. Doctors now have devices that image, visualize, and intervene. CT scans, MRIs, and ultrasounds are frontline tools. Interventions can now be done through tiny incisions just large enough to admit a catheter or the long tube of some type of scope, or – for some procedures – done with no incision at all. Now, perhaps because of this progress, it seems we often leave something behind. Consider the early stethoscope, a wooden instrument that brought doctor and patient within six inches of one another. In their offices, doctors sit facing screens and typing into electronic medical records rather than talking directly to the patient. Tablets are used in a hospital setting to record notes at the bedside. Typing has replaced the spoken word.

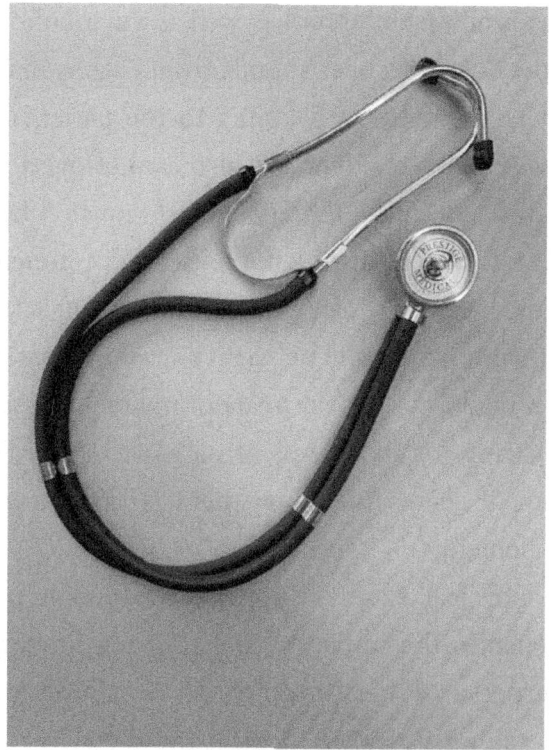

Littman modern stethoscope

Journals have published articles proposing that with new technological advances, the stethoscope is no longer useful; that it is an archaic tool. They say that it belongs in a museum, not in the doctor's grey coat pocket. A colleague told me he had seen a stethoscope mounted and exhibited in a glass case in the office of the chief of radiology at a prestigious university hospital. It was captioned "Historical Relic."

Rather than being a relic, the stethoscope remains a compass, guiding the physician throughout his / her career. It is an essential tool as well as a symbolic one. It allows the doctor to hear sounds from organs inside the body. It is symbolic of listening to the patient's story, and thus remains relevant. We also cannot overlook the role of this tool in the therapeutic relationship between doctor and patient through the sense of touch. The "laying on of hands" during the physical exam is the first step in forming the bond between doctor and patient.

Thinking back over the years of my medical training and of caring for thousands of patients as a practicing physician, it seems that now there is often a missing human element.

The physical exam is a two-way human process, which enables the initiation and ongoing nurturing of an interpersonal relationship. As a young medical student, taking a detailed medical and social history and performing the physical examination often felt very uncomfortable and intrusive. It required breaking the usual barriers of personal space. I memorized the template for the history and physical examination, which helped me concentrate on the feelings that the process generated for both the patient and me. This created the opportunity for me to learn about each patient as an individual and enhanced our bond. There was an implied commitment between the patient and me: that I would use all my skills to care for them, and that the patient would listen and work with me to achieve optimal results. We became partners in the care delivery process.

In a sense, my childhood experience was my own first clinical story. My pediatrician served as a model of what bedside doctoring could look and feel like. My experience of being the patient also showed me how I could best give care in my future as a doctor: my pediatrician had a reassuring tone and warm touch. I felt listened to and treated with respect even though I was only seven years old. The experience left me feeling cared for, even seventy years later.

2

IN THE BEGINNING – LEARNING THE BIBLE

The end of the second year of med school was a time of transition in my medical training. It was exciting to realize that I would now be working with patients. Gone were the days of hours spent in the laboratory or library. Focus now shifted from the intense study of core basic science subjects such as Anatomy, Physiology and Pathology to the clinical practice of bedside medicine. While book learning was essential to understanding the human body in health and disease, it took place in a classroom, divorced from real-time human contact. It did not provide me, the student, even limited exposure to the skills involved in the hands-on patient care. Students would now begin to participate directly in clinical patient care and assume responsibility for real people. This was both exciting and intimidating.

The first step in this transition was learning how to draw out a focused clinical history and perform a thorough physical examination. In doing this, the student would, for the first time, have direct personal interaction with a patient. For weeks, everyone in my class had been studying a book affectionately referred to as the "Blue Book." This book, our Bible, with its deep blue cover, had been written by two faculty professors at the University of Michigan Medical School. It methodically laid out how to engage a patient in a dialogue, from which the doctor would learn a detailed medical history and described how to perform a complete physical examination.

The patient's history would begin with a description of the current problem for which the patient was seeking care. It would progress to questions about the patient's past medical history such as any prior major illnesses or surgeries. Then there would be a broad discussion to unearth any subtle medical issues involving various body systems, such as the cardiovascular, respiratory system, digestive tract, and urinary tract functions. There would follow questions regarding allergies as well as past family and social events. By the time the history was complete, the student doctor would have a good basic understanding of the medical situation he / she was dealing with. The Blue Book similarly tutored the student in how to examine the human body using the basic tools of sight, hearing, touch, and occasionally smell. It taught how to use the stethoscope to listen to various organs, with attention especially to the heart as well as the lungs, bowel, and blood vessels. It taught how to feel for organ enlargement or tenderness. In this way, the Blue Book described a discipline that literally evaluated the patient from head to toe, methodically constructing a mental image of his or her physical health.

Earlier in the day, I had walked up the steps of the university hospital, an imposing and austere large gray stone building. Although I had been in the hospital several times before, it felt unfamiliar and different now. It was as if, for the first time, I was opening a mysterious door that was the entrance to a strange and unknown room. My short white coat marked my position as a student doctor, the lowest in the pecking order. It contrasted with the long white coats worn by more advanced resident trainees and the gray coats of the attending physicians. This was a code known to all hospital staff. It designated to them that I was an uninitiated medical student.

I struggled to repress feelings of self-consciousness, and even more so, the feeling of being an imposter. *Does my insecurity show?* I wondered. But there was excitement too, since I knew this was, at last, the beginning of my transition from neophyte to full-fledged doctor. Clearly, this transition would be gradual and a very intense learning experience. But with it would come increasing clinical involvement and understanding.

Not surprisingly, medical students' inexperience often made their interactions proceed more slowly than those with the experienced physicians – and for this reason, many patients came to value medical student visits. These provided much appreciated human contact in an environment where, it was otherwise, sometimes in short supply.

As I walked through the cavernous hospital halls toward the room of my first patient, I knew none of this, and my trepidation only increased. On reaching the designated room, I hesitated. Then, gathering my thoughts, I knocked on the door and after an appropriate pause, walked in.

The room was dark. The shades had been pulled completely down, creating a somber atmosphere. A sense of sadness and despair was pervasive. It felt as if I had, for the first time, entered the strange and previously unknown world of illness.

In bed was a young woman thirty-eight years of age. She was lying on her back with her blanket pulled up to and under her chin. Her pallor was striking. She had lost much of her hair.

I was momentarily stunned! It had never occurred to me that my first patient, Lynn, would be a young woman with breast cancer. It was 1969, and in that era, the word "cancer" was spoken only in whispers. There was, in fact, a stigma associated with having cancer, as if those afflicted had done something to bring a curse upon themselves.

Lynn's bed was positioned parallel to the length of the room, and there was a ledge along the inside wall. After I introduced myself, I walked into the room, passed the foot of the bed and sat down on this ledge, facing her. Once again, I fought my discomfort, and tried as hard as I could to appear at ease in this unfamiliar atmosphere. Since performing my first medical history and physical examination would be a deliberate process, I hoped that positioning myself deep in her room would convey that she would be the focus of this interaction, that it would be unrushed, and that I would be fully engaged. I explained to Lynn that in taking her history I would be asking her a series of questions that she quite likely had been asked many times before, but that this was an important part of my job as a medical student doctor.

Having memorized the basic template for a history and physical examination from the Blue Book, I was reassured. It provided a format for what was a totally unfamiliar interaction. Being conscious of this helped ease my trepidation. My goal was to project competence and gain Lynn's trust even in the face of my lack of prior experience.

The interview began with a series of short questions that were easily answered. She was a thirty-eight-year-old white female, married with three children. But despite my best efforts, my sense of anxiety persisted. I was a young man in my early twenties. Lynn was relatively close in age. She could have been my older sister or cousin. The scar from her recent surgery was still healing. The skin on either side of it was discolored and taut. Mastectomy surgery was disfiguring. Although I consciously tried to appear composed, I feared that my discomfort was evident.

Lynn was a music teacher by profession. Gradually my tension decreased. As the interview progressed, the exchanges became more conversational. She became more at ease and my presence ceased to feel intrusive.

Why had she come to the hospital?
What was her problem and how long had she known of it?
What were her symptoms and what was their intensity?
Was she having pain?
How long ago had the diagnosis been made, and how?

As this process continued and both of us became more relaxed, her answers were less constrained. But when we moved to the physical examination, my sense of awkwardness returned.

She was young to have been diagnosed with metastatic breast cancer. She had recently undergone radical mastectomy and radiation therapy. Further treatment was scheduled after she recovered from her recent surgery. She was wearing a typical hospital gown. This was made from soft, thin material that draped loosely over her torso and lower body. It had two openings in its upper portion with short sleeves that allowed her arms full movement. The gown wrapped her loosely from her neck to knees. It was held in place by two cloth ties that secured the gown formlessly around her. Whatever sense of style Lynn may have had in her former life had been stolen by this hospital gown.

Not even the revered Blue Book or any amount of study could have prepared me for the next moments. I felt consciously aware of her modesty and carefully kept her covered to avoid embarrassing either of us. I proceeded deliberately with her physical examination. Her skin was cool and pale. I warmed the head of the stethoscope in my hands before placing it on her back and over her lungs. The chest scar from her mastectomy was not yet fully healed so I was particularly careful not to put pressure on it as I listened to her heart.

Lynn's examination progressed slowly but systematically:

Head to toe
Nervous system and orientation
Eyes, ears, nose, and throat
Neck including thyroid gland and lymph nodes
Lungs
Heart
Abdomen
Legs, ankles, and feet – temperature, color, swelling and pulses

After completing her formal history and physical exam, we paused momentarily. Somewhat to my surprise, she redirected our conversation back again to her social history and current family situation. Lynn seemed to crave the opportunity to talk more about her family. She was the mother of three young children, the oldest being nine years old. Her illness was causing marked family disruption, particularly since her husband's job required frequent travel. Her oldest child, Amy, loved music and was studying piano.

"My daughter has a gift for the piano. She has given several recitals despite her young age," she said. "My middle child, David, is studying the violin and advancing nicely," she continued. "And my five-year-old daughter, Pamela, loves to draw and will soon begin weekly art classes geared to her age group."

Lynn continued, explaining that her whole family loved hiking and being outdoors. They had taken several camping trips together. Obviously though, their lives had changed dramatically with the sudden onset of her illness.

I listened, becoming pensive. Here was a young mother facing what would likely become a death sentence. She was at an age that would have been expected to be early years of a fulfilling and rewarding personal and family life. Clearly, her illness was tragic not only for her, but for her husband and three children. They would quite possibly be by default, abruptly deprived of a wife and mother. It was unnerving.

At the conclusion of my prescribed tasks, I lingered so we could speak a bit further. During our conversations, Lynn related that most of her physicians seemed hurried and distant when they visited her, often staying in her room only briefly. She was frequently seen only by the junior member of her care team, while the other team members stood talking just outside of her door. At times, she said, she would be in her room for hours without seeing or speaking with another person.

I later learned that in this era, it was not unusual for physicians to view care of any cancer patient as a personal failure, since effective treatments for many types of cancers simply did not exist. Somehow caring for cancer patients, with little hope for survival, was experienced as a reminder of the limits of the doctor's healing powers.

For this reason, as in this case, interactions with a

cancer patient were often medically correct but devoid of social conversation, often delegated to the most junior physician on the team. As our conversation moved on, Lynn shared with me more vignettes of her career as a music teacher, and of each of her three children, and of how she had previously juggled career with the responsibilities of motherhood. It was easy to empathize with her, and at the same time to feel a twinge of angst. Her situation spoke not only to her vulnerability, but to the vulnerability of every young family to unanticipated medical crises.

Because of our spontaneous conversation, I stayed far longer than anticipated. When I finally rose to leave, Lynn's affect changed. She appeared momentarily lost in thought.

And then she said, "Promise me that you will come back and see me again."

Hiding my surprise, I promised that I would.

Four months passed. The first two months were spent as the junior medical student with one of the university's surgical teams. The experience was demanding and filled with intense learning. Medical students were expected to carry out a variety of clinical and supportive tasks required for patient care. While in today's hospitals, computers make clinical information such as laboratory test results available for review with a keystroke or touch of a smart phone screen, these time-saving tools were not yet even a fantasy.

A typical day began at dawn with the student drawing patient blood samples for laboratory tests and filling out the individual paper request forms that accompanied these samples to the laboratory. Striving for efficiency, students were taught to use a small laboratory on the ward to perform straightforward postoperative tests such as blood counts. Additionally, they collected the paper forms with results of tests done the evening or afternoon before. Students were required to have them ready for the senior doctor on the team to review. Since digital imaging was not yet available, students also retrieved, and later returned, pertinent postoperative X-ray films.

The medical student usually arrived at the hospital to begin these tasks at 6:00 a.m. so that they would be complete when the main surgical team arrived. At 6:30 a.m., the team made rounds, reviewing the status of each patient and any changes in condition from the prior afternoon or evening. Particular attention was focused on those who had most recently had surgical procedures. The first operations of the day would then begin at 7:30 a.m., and I usually joined the team for the procedure in the operating room. On most days the team had two or more operations to perform. The last of these would be completed at any time from late morning on into the afternoon, depending on the complexity of the day's operations. The remaining afternoon and often evening was spent taking admitting histories and physical examinations on new patients whose operations were scheduled for the following day.

We also did clinical errands requested by the senior physicians. Frequently, the planned order of the day would suddenly be revised to accommodate emergencies or unexpected complications. And on a revolving schedule, one surgical team would remain in the hospital overnight, a thirty-six-hour shift, to deal with any emergency or trauma patient that was admitted.

My two months on the surgical team were days both exhilarating and exhausting. The intense learning that occurred through watching, assisting, and discussing the wide range of surgical problems made the long days fly by. When the first month of this rotation was completed, I had taken medical histories and done physical examinations on several dozens of patients. I had helped in the OR as a basic, non-technical assistant, typically holding instruments (retractors) that helped expose the surgical operative field. I had participated in the care of patients with a range of surgical problems.

The hurried pace of these days, and the fact that I was doing this rotation once again at the University Hospital, allowed me to revisit Lynn, my very first patient. Most days I managed a visit to her, in essence putting her on my patient rounds list. It became apparent that the time spent with her allowed for social interactions and support. I learned that even as a medical student, my visits added meaning and comfort for both of us. It was the first time that I realized that even with my inexperience, I could make a difference. She enjoyed these visits and soon looked forward to them and so did I. There were also occasions where I could help her get the attention of the nurses' aides or the nurses themselves instead of waiting for her call button to be answered. I came to realize that hospitalized patients often spent hours alone each day with little human contact. Surgeons spent hours in the operating room with a sleeping patient. Their follow-up post-op visits were often brief. Sometimes the only personal conversations the patient had all day were with the cleaning or dietary staff.

One afternoon, after I had been on the surgical team for several weeks, Lynn had some news to share.

"I'm scheduled to be discharged and go home at the end of this week. The Chief said I had healed adequately to leave but needed some additional time off before my next radiation treatment."

"Will you need help at home with the chores and in caring for your kids?" I asked.

"I'm not sure how that will go," she answered. "My husband hasn't been able to travel for his job as he usually does, and I was hoping to be able to manage myself so that he could start to keep up with those assignments," she said.

"Let me see if a request for a consultation from Social Services was sent," I offered, and with that I spoke to the admin covering the surgical service caring for Lynn. The admin agreed to call the team and request permission to place a consultation. Lynn was visibly relieved when I told her that Social Services would arrange for some help at home.

"If you are readmitted after next month, most likely I'll be on a service at the County or VA hospital," I said. "I don't know if I'll have the chance to see you again. Good luck."

We both had enjoyed our visits, although for different reasons. It was a bit sad to realize that each of us had to move on. I finished my time on the surgical service and moved along onto the Adult Medicine service at the Cook County Hospital. On occasion I had to be at the University Hospital for administrative reasons or brief assignments, and at first, I checked patient lists to see if by chance Lynn was in the hospital, but our paths didn't cross.

Like the Surgical service, the Adult Medicine assignment was an intense learning experience. It was also extremely demanding. Most of my days started early and went late into the night – if, in fact, I didn't stay overnight in the hospital. I had responsibilities for many patients, both new admissions with complex medical or surgical problems and some people with more chronic problems. My initial introduction to the art of history taking and doing physical examinations seemed far in the past.

Six months passed.

During various rotations, students attended lectures or short courses in several medical subspecialties. Since these focused on discrete areas of the major disciplines, at this stage of medical education it was considered essential for students to focus for longer periods on broader, more general areas of clinical medicine, rather than on specialties. And so it happened that one afternoon, following a busy overnight stay in the hospital, I walked into a lecture hall and sat down as the professor was about to begin. His topic was the challenges of dealing with terminally ill patients and those in the last phases of their disease. He had videotaped an interview with such a patient earlier in the week.

I slumped down in my chair, fighting my fatigue, and trying to stay awake.

A woman was speaking. Even on the videotape, it was apparent that she was thin, pale, and had lost virtually all her hair. Her story was compelling. She had felt a lump in her left breast and at essentially the same time also felt a nodule under her left arm. She had quickly sought medical attention and had been sent for a biopsy. Not surprisingly, the biopsy demonstrated breast cancer. She had subsequently undergone mastectomy followed by radiation and chemotherapy. She had recently been hospitalized with widespread metastases.

As she explained her story, I became more alert despite my fatigue.

She said, "It is very difficult to deal with a diagnosis like this, especially when you are young and anticipated having many more years to live." She then continued, "When you begin treatment, you end up spending many long hours in your hospital room alone. One of the hardest things to deal with is the many hours between visits from the doctors. It is as if with the cancer diagnosis you have become an *untouchable*. The isolation becomes very depressing."

I sat up and focused. "There was one student doctor. He visited me regularly and spent time talking to me. It meant the world to me that he visited me frequently, as he had promised. I came to look forward to his visits." I sat up in my seat, stunned. I recognized that the woman was Lynn. She had aged considerably. Her hair had thinned, her skin tone was cachectic, and her voice was softer. She appeared very frail.

It was true that I had visited Lynn frequently when her hospitalizations overlapped my clinical assignments, but it never occurred to me that these visits had been so significant to her. I had incorrectly assumed that because I was a medical student beginning to learn bedside care, my visits lacked import. Her words led me to rethink their impact. Lynn's sense of isolation was palpable. The fact that I did what I had promised had meaning to her.

Her words affirmed that the human connection in medical care added an important dimension beyond what could be learned in textbooks. What mattered the most to Lynn was my humanity, not the extent of my training.

The reliable visits had helped ease Lynn's sense of isolation and loneliness. I too had benefitted greatly, as I realized that even this early on in training, I could make a difference, a human difference.

3

AMBULANCE RIDE, JERUSALEM

By chance an ambulance pulled up outside of the Emergency Room just as I reached the hospital entrance.

Why do the ambulance's sirens still shake me up so much? I asked myself.

It's like I'm still there. I can still hear the mob screaming, I said, answering my own question.

* * *

Israel, summer of 1968. This was one year after a surprise preemptive strike by the Israeli Air Force that set the stage for the rapid and decisive victory over the surrounding hostile Arab states of Jordan, Egypt, and Syria. They had amassed troops on their respective borders with Israel and with increasing frequency announced their intent to annihilate the young nation.

I was beginning my fourth year of medical school and had decided to take an elective rotation in surgery in Israel. To do so in a foreign country, the site of ancient cultures and at the same time modern in its medical practices, was appealing. I was able to arrange a rotation at an Israeli hospital located in the historic city of Jerusalem.

The hospital, Shaare Tzedek, whose name meant "Gates of Righteousness," had been built in a converted British Taggart Fort. This rectangular stone structure had been constructed around 1940, during British colonial days, when it served as a base for police and military operations.

Jerusalem itself was a fascinating mosaic of religions, cultures, customs, and architecture. It had grown outward around the ancient walled city that dated to Biblical times and housed sites sacred to the Muslim, Christian, and Jewish religions.

The Surgical training rotation provided some interesting contrasts to my prior clinical experiences. Although the quality of care was similar to that in the United States, equipment and supplies were, in general, not as new nor as readily available. The building itself was also not as polished as the University hospital in the States. There was marked contrast between the Surgery Service's organizational structure and that of the American Service. The conspicuous hierarchical culture at home was replaced by a much less formal and quite collegial structure at all levels. I was quickly made to feel welcome and like my contributions to daily operations were appreciated.

Clinical responsibilities were completed by mid-afternoon, and it was always fascinating to explore the Old City.

Although I was somewhat aware of the prevailing social climate, I was largely unaware of the tension created by the war and the new political reality. Before the Six-Day War the previous year, Jerusalem had been partitioned according to armistice borders drawn at the positions of the Jordanian and Israeli armies when the Israeli War of Independence ended in 1948.

The Old City, ancient and walled, and the contiguous eastern sections, had been under Jordanian Arab control; the newer western areas were predominantly Israeli. However, as a result of the Six-Day War both the Old City and East Jerusalem had again come under Israeli governance. The net effect was that although the war had ended, there was underlying tension between the two populations.

Things went smoothly for my first two weeks. The days were filled with meaningful surgical experience as well as wonderful opportunities to explore and understand the country's rich history.

One night, the calm was suddenly broken by the

concussion of a loud explosion nearby. *Oh my God.* I was confused and scared. "What happened?" The quiet evening had been shattered by the attack. No one realized that this would be the beginning of a repetitive cycle of terror followed by retaliation. Peace had been disrupted.

Several days later, we learned that a lone Arab man had detonated a hand grenade in a very busy and popular open-air market and bazaar. This bazaar was in the Israeli section of the new city but was frequented daily by all segments of Jerusalem's residents. It sold all manner of foods: meats, nuts, dried fruits, vegetables, oils, olives, spices, and breads, as well as an eclectic array of household items and goods ranging from hand-woven rugs to small decorative items.

The room where I lived was several blocks from this market. I heard the jarring explosion. It didn't take long to learn through the grapevine that there had been a terrorist attack. Rumors circulated that at least several persons had been injured and were being rushed to the Shaare Tzedek Emergency Room for surgical treatment of their wounds. My reaction to this news was immediate and reflexive. Although I had never thought about it in these terms before, Shaare Tzedek had become "my" hospital. A brisk walk brought me there where I proceeded directly to the locker rooms adjacent to the operating rooms. The surgeons and staff had already returned and were setting up to receive the wounded.

They had hurriedly changed from street clothes to surgical scrubs and were busy organizing their approach to the trauma situation. They added their own level of triage to the initial triage done in the ER.

"You came back!" One of the surgeons said to me. He seemed both surprised and pleased. "I'm glad you're here. We're going to need all the help we can mobilize."

"I figured that with multiple injuries the system would be stressed. This is where I belong," I replied.

Several shoppers walking through the bazaar had been hit by shrapnel and sustained wounds that would require surgical exploration and repair. I was about to change to go to the OR when the Chief Surgeon approached me after having a short, intense conversation with one of the ER nurses.

"Jay," he began. "We have a problem. We're at full capacity, overflowing with the wounded. We're going to operate on those who need immediate help. There's an Arab man, about sixty years old, who was also injured by the grenade. The ambulance brought him to the ER here. He's been stabilized and is getting IV fluids, but he needs to go to the OR. As I said, the OR and staff are maxed out. I think he would be best served by transfer to an Arab hospital in East Jerusalem. I called over there. They still have the space and staff to take care of him. I need you to accompany him in the ambulance."

Had I known what the ambulance ride would entail, I probably still would have agreed, but with foreknowledge and more trepidation. In a few minutes, an ambulance from the East Jerusalem hospital arrived, the man's gurney and IVs were secured, and the two of us were moved into the waiting vehicle. By this time, the wounded man had received one full liter of fluids and was starting his second. He was pale, with a modestly increased heart rate and blood pressure marginally above the shock level. His skin was damp and slightly cool. All these signs reflected his need for early intervention.

The ambulance bore markings and signage that identified it as being from an Arab hospital. In short order, with sirens blaring and lights flashing, we left Shaare Tzedek's ER on what should have been a ten-minute ride. I was unaware that we needed to cross an invisible Arab-Israeli boundary in the city.

A crowd had formed around the ER driveway as we prepared to depart for the East Jerusalem hospital. We had gone several blocks when the crowd grew larger and more agitated. Angry protesters tried to encircle us. "Murderer, murderer!" They chanted. People pounded the side of the ambulance with their fists.

Whenever the vehicle slowed, several people started trying to rock it. Their shouts suggested they thought that our passenger was the terrorist grenade thrower. At times, the extreme narrowing of the streets slowed our progress to a crawl.

The crowd grew. We found ourselves drawn deeper

and deeper into the middle of an angry mob. I opened one of the ambulance's upper windows a couple of inches tried to yell back. "He's a victim, he's not the terrorist!" I yelled in Hebrew. The crowd most likely couldn't hear me, but if they did, my words were to no avail. A man grabbed the ambulance's back handle and tried to open the door. Fortunately, it had an inside lock that had been secured.

Enraged, he loudly demanded that we let him take the patient and turn him over to the mob. He kept shouting as he ran alongside the ambulance, "Give him to us! Give him to us now!"

Another shouting match ensued. Once again, I tried "explaining" that this patient had no responsibility for the explosion.

"He didn't do it! He's not the terrorist!" I shouted again and again. *Why couldn't they understand that he was, in fact, one of the victims?* My attempts at reason were, not surprisingly, unheeded. Luckily, although the shouting continued and angry people still ran alongside us, we steadily made progress. As we approached the East Jerusalem hospital, a police escort materialized, and the crowd finally disbursed.

Several nurses and a doctor were waiting for us at the ER entrance. They secured our patient's IVs and carefully transferred him from the ambulance to the hospital's gurney.

"Shaare Tzedek's ORs are full," I said by way of

explanation. "Thank you for taking him." The receiving doctor nodded and assessed his vital signs and wounds. "An operating room has been reserved for him," the receiving doctor said. "We've been waiting. He'll go there directly."

I sighed in relief. The patient had been safely delivered. The ambulance driver took me back to Shaare Tzedek where I rejoined the team caring for the wounded. Operating went on well into the night.

It was naive to expect an angry mob would accept that all patients have the right to medical care. This was implicit in our training, but rarely tested.

4

LEARNING FROM EXPERIENCE

The fourth year of medical school, after my return from an elective in Israel, was a milestone I anticipated with excitement. I would be working as a sub-intern at a county hospital in suburban Detroit under the supervision of a medical resident. County hospital rotations required the student to carry greater patient responsibility, in both diagnosis and treatment, than was typical at the University Hospital. This was in part due to a chronic shortage of physicians assigned to county facilities.

I met the medical resident I would be working with, Dr. Mark, for the first time at the beginning of the rotation. He and I cared for a group of fifteen to twenty adult patients hospitalized with a wide range of non-surgical illnesses: heart or kidney failure, cancer of any type, or a variety of infections. Patient diversity meant that it was quite unusual to care for two patients with similar diagnoses at the same time.

Dr. Mark's rotation had started a few days before mine, so he was already familiar with our patients when I began working with him. We had been on service together about two weeks when a new patient, Mr. Lee came under our care. Mr. Lee was in his late sixties. He was small in stature and appeared frail. He had lost twenty pounds over the past three months, but until that point, he had been well. Recently, he had lost his appetite and experienced marked fatigue and generalized weakness. When I examined him, the only abnormality I could find other than his fragility was a prominent lymph node in the axilla area under his right arm. The node was fixed in place, round, and about one half inch in diameter. Other laboratory tests and a routine X-rays of his chest and abdomen were normal. After Dr. Mark and I had each taken Mr. Lee's history and examined him, we sat down to discuss his case.

"I would think that with his generalized fatigue, weakness and weight loss, some type of cancer is the most likely underlying problem," I said.

"That would seem probable. Did you find any evidence of it? If Mr. Lee does have a cancer, were there any clues to what type of cancer it might be or what the primary origin is?"

"The only abnormal physical finding I picked up was

the prominent lymph node under his right arm," I answered.

"What would you suggest we do next? How would you proceed?" Dr. Mark asked.

"A biopsy of that lymph node would most likely be helpful. I would expect it may identify the cell type and probable origin of his cancer."

Dr. Mark agreed, and we decided that I would consult the general surgery resident. If he agreed, we would ask him to schedule a lymph node biopsy as soon as feasible.

After we finished our morning rounds, I paged the surgical resident and requested that he consult on Mr. Lee and schedule a lymph node biopsy. Our treatment would almost certainly depend on the pathology findings from this biopsy. At the minimum, it would narrow the possibilities and suggest how next to proceed.

At the time, CT scanning and MRI, which in today's medical practice often provide direct answers, were not yet available. In any case, Dr. Mark and I thought a biopsy would be necessary.

It happened that the surgical resident was in the OR and involved in a long, difficult case. I didn't get a return call from him until late that afternoon, when I presented Mr. Lee's case and requested that he schedule the biopsy for the following day. Unfortunately, the OR schedule was already full. The earliest the biopsy could be done was in two days.

I paged Dr. Mark to update him. "The OR schedule is full for the next couple of days. The earliest opening is the day after tomorrow."

Dr. Mark was frustrated by the unexpected delay. "We can't move ahead without that information. We can't have him spend an extra two days in the hospital. Let's do the biopsy ourselves. The wards are crowded. We need to move patients along."

I'm not convinced. I thought, filling with trepidation. *I hope he knows what he is doing!*

Surprised and unnerved by this suggestion, I was moved to speak up. "Have you done any biopsies or similar surgical procedures before?" I asked.

"The node is just under the skin – it should be easy to get the tissue sample. It can't be that difficult."

I still wasn't convinced. I protested one more time, though in retrospect, not as strongly as I might have. Dr. Mark said, "I heard you," and then, ignoring my voiced concern, asked the nurse for the surgical tools and supplies he would need. We went into Mr. Lee's room and told him that we planned to biopsy the node under his arm. He consented, although our explanation was superficial.

The procedure appeared to go well. We made a small skin incision over the lymph node. The node was readily accessible, and we got the tissue samples we wanted without apparent difficulty. We applied pressure to the incision in Mr. D's armpit for several minutes. At that point no further bleeding was apparent. Finally, the three-quarter inch skin incision was sutured closed. We spent the remainder of the afternoon finishing rounds and attending to the other patients. By 4:30 p.m. we had only a few more details to address.

Abruptly, Dr. Mark's pager went off. A few seconds later my pager went off.

Together we hurried to Mr. Lee's room. He was sitting upright in the chair in the corner. His hospital gown was stained red, beginning immediately under his right arm, and extending down all the way to his waist. The red stain covered a progressively widening area as it moved further from his under-arm. The nurse had started a large IV in his left arm immediately after she paged us. *Could all that blood be coming from such a small incision?*

The surgical resident had also been urgently paged. He arrived only a few moments after Dr. Mark and I did. Together we assisted Mr. Lee back to bed and helped him lie flat. The surgical resident quickly sterilized the incision and adjacent area, making a sterile field surrounding it. Using the pointed tip of a scalpel blade he cut the sutures holding the incision closed and wiped away the blood. In an instant the answer became clear. A small branch of an artery lay just beneath the skin's surface. It was no larger in diameter than a piece of string. With each heartbeat, several drops of blood spurted out and into the surrounding area. While the amount of blood ejected with each beat was small, over time the volume of blood loss became significant.

The surgical resident quickly isolated the offending small artery branch and tied it closed with a length of fine suture. When he was satisfied that no further bleeding would occur, he again sutured the skin incision closed and dressed the wound. We stepped outside the patient's room and walked into the hall.

The surgical resident looked directly at Dr. Mark and then at me. "It's obvious you guys didn't check your patient post-op," he said somewhat sarcastically. "Stick to medicine and leave surgery to the surgeons. I'll check him once more in a couple hours."

I was relieved this had not happened in the middle of the night with no surgeon available.

Dr. Mark and I ordered lab tests to determine Mr. Lee's blood count later that evening.

No further bleeding occurred, but our patient was ultimately transfused two units of red blood cells. The biopsy results led to a diagnosis of colon cancer. He went on to have surgery followed by chemotherapy. A week later he was discharged home for outpatient follow-up.

* * *

Mr. Lee's case taught me several lessons. I realized that to learn from untoward outcomes or unforeseen complications, I needed to critically review my own decision-making process. It was imperative to determine how, when, and why the mistakes had been made. Although this could be done alone, it was helpful to have input from colleagues. In this case, I questioned both my judgment and strategy, while recognizing that there was a clear authority hierarchy. The ultimate decision-maker, with the patient's consent, of course, was the patient's attending physician or the most senior physician on the case. Here, Dr. Mark was that person. Doctors might disagree, debate, or even argue, but ultimately the physician at the top of the pyramid had final say.

In Mr. Lee's case, scheduling his node biopsy myself when I spoke to the surgical resident might have made a difference. It would have been legitimate for me to schedule the biopsy at the earliest available OR opening in an attempt to facilitate Mr. Lee's care. Then, Dr. Mark might not have undertaken the biopsy. It would have required him to actively change the schedule that I had already put in place.

I also wondered if I had pushed back hard enough on Dr. Mark. My protests had clearly annoyed him, but they were ineffective. I had no way of judging his surgical competence, but I could have politely explored this and perhaps led him to reconsider. It was reasonable for me to ask him if he had ever performed any lymph node biopsies; instead of giving me a direct answer, he projected a confidence I assumed was based on prior experience. There would be cases in the future in which my medical judgment prevailed over that of more senior colleagues. Each case would be unique, and my clinical judgment would likewise be based on prior experience, the only guide I had. Going ahead and scheduling Mr. Lee's biopsy based on my assessment and conversation with the surgical resident, probably would have made Dr. Mark's overconfident, rogue approach less likely because it would have required him to contradict my scheduling rather than requiring me to convince him to change his plan.

There was a final, perhaps most important lesson in this case, and one I would carry through thirty years of practice. I would revisit every patient on whom I had performed a procedure, shortly after completing it and again at the end of the day, before leaving the hospital. Doing follow-up visits helped assure patient safety and prevent complications. Follow-up visits after a procedure were beneficial to both the patient and me. They enhanced patient safety and gave me peace of mind.

PART II

INTERNSHIP AND RESIDENCY, 1971–1975

5

TEAMWORK

It was early July, and my internship was just beginning. This was the first year I would spend caring for hospitalized patients, a doctor with primary care responsibility. It was an exciting time. I had just graduated from medical school and reached a proud milestone in my career. I felt at the top of my game, proud of my achievement. I had not yet experienced the numbing exhaustion that would soon come from sleepless nights on call. My first assignment was to care for patients in the Coronary Care Unit (CCU).

The ward clerk, Millie, saw me and motioned for me to come over.

"I need to see you," she said somewhat earnestly.

Her desk and workspace were located centrally at the beginning of two adjacent hallways. Each hallway led to the entrances to fifteen patient rooms.

"Do you need something?" I asked when I neared her desk. "By the way, are the blood test results on my patients back from the lab yet?"

"No, Doc," she said, "the blood for your patients' lab tests didn't get drawn this morning."

I was surprised. "I filled out the requisitions in plenty of time for them to be processed," I said. *I need that information to make the best decisions for my patients.*

I had assumed that lab work ordered the night before would be done by the following morning. I could get by without the information, but this was not optimal.

This was many years before computerized information systems were developed. The blood tests a patient needed were requisitioned by filling out a special paper slip. Tests were grouped on these slips according to the body functions they assessed. Small boxes preceded the listing of each test, and we indicated what was needed by marking the box next to the test name.

Millie handed me the small stack of lab requisition slips I had filled out the night before.

"These are yours," she said a bit sheepishly. I looked at each of the slips in the group. My choice of tests seemed appropriate. I had indeed checked the boxes next to those tests that the patients needed and would not have expected the lab to edit or deny my choices in any case.

"They look OK to me," I offered. I was a bit confused,

but handed them back to her and asked, "Wasn't the lab supposed to draw the blood samples for these this morning? Maybe something called the tech away and she forgot to come back. Let's try again for later today."

Millie reached out and took the slips back. She gave me a strange look and started to say something, but just then my pager went off.

By the time I had answered the call and dealt with the issue, I had pretty much moved on from the earlier conversation. Additionally, the shift had changed, and Millie left for the day. As far as I knew, my requisitions would have been resubmitted and done midday, and the results would be available by late afternoon. I would like to have received the information earlier for the day's morning patient visits, but I would make do. *I'll double back later in the day. The results should be available by then*, I said to myself.

I revisited the floor later in the afternoon, but no results had come back. I was on call that same night and had multiple new admissions. Several of the patients had been gravely ill, and there was no time to sleep. I was exhausted and anxious to attend to the day's business efficiently. I would be on call again the following night – if I finished my work and got home quickly, I could catch an hour or two more of sleep.

The next morning, I returned to Millie's desk to collect the lab reports. I was about to make morning rounds and see how everyone had fared overnight.

"Good morning, Millie. Are my lab results back yet?" Millie looked distressed as I approached. I soon found out why. She hesitated for a moment before beginning.

"I wanted to tell you yesterday, but you got paged away and I didn't see you again before I left for the evening," she said.

She handed me a stack of lab requisition slips that was significantly thicker than the prior days. Paper-clipped to the top slip was a small handwritten note that said: "Please fill these out correctly before resubmitting."

I was puzzled to say the least. *What could it possibly mean to fill the slips out "correctly"?*

Millie looked even more uncomfortable. It was quickly becoming clear, at least to her, that she would have to be the one to initiate me into the system. I had indeed checked the boxes indicating the tests required. I picked up a slip and looked at it closely. At the top of each one, a header printed in small font said:

"Please indicate the tests to be done by placing an 'X' in the appropriate box."

I once more looked carefully at the slip I was holding. At about the same time, Millie pointed to the "instructions." Their meaning gradually dawned on me, and I suddenly flushed with irritation. I had marked a check next to the tests I wanted done. A check, and not an X.

I stared in disbelief. I didn't know if I was more stunned, frustrated, or angry.

I need the test results to properly care for my *patients*, I thought. Caring for this group of people with heart attacks and other heart problems was my job. It was my reason for being there! I assumed that it was also the goal of the other people working in the hospital, that we all in fact shared a common purpose.

I was ready to start my daily rounds. These test results were essential. Each patient needed to be carefully evaluated and a treatment plan formulated for the next twenty-four hours of care. The lab information was an integral part of this process. Now, I would have to fill out a new set of requisition slips, putting an X – not a check mark – in the appropriate places.

The lab tech was done for the day so I would need to draw the blood samples myself and take them to the lab. This would add at least an hour or possibly two to my day. I would pay for my mistake with additional hours in the hospital added to the end of my day. The currency for that payment would be lost sleep. And sleep, even this early in the internship, was becoming a highly valued commodity. The look I gave Millie must have conveyed some strong emotions. She looked at me somewhat sheepishly and said, "I tried to tell you but…"

I interrupted, "I'm going to get tests drawn and in process, and then I'm going to have a few words with the laboratory manager." My tone left no doubt that I expected a confrontation. "My purpose is to take care of the patients, not quibble about the difference between 'X' and a check mark," I said forcefully.

The whole "check versus X" episode had spanned a thirty-six-hour period. I was not amused.

When I finished making rounds and the blood samples had been drawn and delivered, I circled back to the laboratory to find and confront the lab manager. The intervening time had not dulled my indignation.

As I approached the lab, I saw a smartly dressed young woman standing by herself and looking at some papers. She appeared to be about thirty-five years old. I approached her and, in a voice devoid of any irritation, asked, "Could you please tell me where I might find the lab manager?"

She looked at me and in an equally pleasant voice answered, "I am the manager."

Somehow, I had anticipated that the manager would be older and more austere-looking.

To say that I was taken aback was a gross understatement. Then she added, "Are you one of the new interns? In fact, are you the intern covering the Coronary Care Unit? I was hoping to see you and thought maybe you would be coming down so I could meet you. It always helps if the new interns have the chance to learn a bit about how we run the laboratory."

I was caught totally off guard. My expectation was that I would unleash a small tirade and give the manager a stern lecture. But somehow, her cordial demeanor and the tone of her short introduction made an angry approach seem inappropriate. In a voice that perhaps conveyed surprise but which must have sounded cordial, I said to her, "I'm Dr. Kleiman. I wanted to meet you and thank you for all the help you've been giving me."

I thought my tone conveyed some irony, if not overt sarcasm, but fortunately that was not what she heard.

"Well, hello," she said. "I'm glad to meet you too. The Coronary Care Unit uses a lot of tests, and sometimes they need results quickly. Please let me know if you have any special testing needs and I'll do my best to help you as much as possible. It's helpful to know who I'm working with."

Over the next several weeks I thought about that episode a great deal. From that moment on I had no more difficulty in working with the lab to get the patient's testing needs addressed efficiently. Somehow, the check versus X episode had leveled the playing field. The personal interaction had created a bridge. I tried to imagine what things looked like from her perspective. New interns rotated through the Coronary Care Unit every one or two months. I wondered how the permanent staff saw us. While laboratory services were used throughout the hospital, the need and demand for them was by far the greatest in the Critical Care Units. Whatever lessons hospital staff wanted the interns to learn had to be repeated by the staff every month or two. This could be a source of tension for both staff and students. By the time one group had been oriented, they moved onto a new rotation and a new group came on board.

Medical school was structured and formal. It was from the beginning a rigorous graduate program typically requiring the completion of four years of college before admission. The schedule was filled with prescribed coursework and the full schedule allowed few electives. Once the student began the clinical rotations, typically in their third and fourth years, the culture was rigid and hierarchic. It was in many ways, oriented toward meeting the doctors' needs, which would then pass through to the patients' benefit, rather than starting out with the patients' needs as primary.

In my four years of study, I had never had any courses or workshops on group dynamics, organizational structure, or teamwork. There were many indicators of a physician's status in the pyramided structure, from the length and color of the lab coat worn to the position in the line of doctors when formal rounds were made. Interns went from being at the top of the ladder at med school graduation to being almost the lowest in ranking, with only the medical students below them. But even as this transition took place, the interns' familiarity with hospital culture and their understanding of their status in this new structure was minimal. Some carried their pride in graduating med school to excess. Add to this the fact that the hospital staff had to deal with new interns every month or two, and it was at least understandable that, on occasion, they had limited patience.

The lab manager kept her word. We became colleagues, interacting cordially and directly several times during the year. There were no further difficulties. The tirade I had expected to deliver was unceremoniously discarded. At the time I didn't quite understand what had happened in that initial face-to-face meeting. The "confrontation" that I had anticipated had never taken place.

I got some understanding of the dynamic later in the year when I was about to start a rotation in the Intensive Care Unit (ICU). I happened to talk with the intern, Steve, who was just finishing his time there.

"You may well not like it," Steve said. "The nurses can be very intimidating and impatient, even though some of what you'll be doing will be new to you." I decided to try something.

Early on the morning when I began my ICU rotation, I asked one of the nurses who the head nurse was. I walked over to her and introduced myself.

"Good morning," I began. "I'm Dr. Kleiman and I'll be the intern working with you this month. I'm really looking forward to it. I understand that it's a great learning experience." I finished with a smile and left.

It was, in fact, a great learning experience. The nurses were reliably helpful and always anxious to share the lessons they had learned through months and years of practice in caring for very sick patients. I gradually came to understand how every part of the team played a key role in delivering coordinated care to each patient. The intern was only one part of the team and had not yet learned the rules of the game. For the team to function as intended, everyone had to play their part and play by the rules. Having never played on a team, only in a high school orchestra, I took a while to adjust. Years later, when I led a team in the cath lab, and ran a cardiology practice, I needed those tools to get members to work together, each bringing their own skills and coordinating for the best patient care.

6

PERSUASION

It was 12:30 a.m. I'd probably been asleep about a half an hour. The call came for me to see a patient in the Emergency Room. I fought my way awake through a nauseating, dense fog of sleep. It was months since I had slept through two nights in a row. I tried to clear my head, and then staggered down four flights of stairs and through the isolated hall. Two wide metal electric double doors opened as I approached, swallowing me into the cavernous ER.

The patient, Eddie, was a middle-aged Black man with a red, hot, swollen, and exquisitely tender knee. He moved slowly and with a pronounced limp. His temperature was close to 102.6. His arms bore telltale track marks of IV drug use. It was probable that his knee was infected, the resting place of bacterial contamination from a dirty needle.

I looked at my watch. Even working efficiently, I'd be lucky to get back to bed by 4:30 or 5:00 a.m. to catch a few hours of sleep before morning rounds at 7:30 a.m. The ER was empty, so Eddie's evaluation and initial treatment could be started there. Otherwise, it would take an hour or more for him to move through the admitting process, up to the ward, and through the initial nursing procedures.

I ran through a mental checklist. In addition to a history and physical examination, Eddie would need blood tests, blood cultures, an ECG and X-rays. His knee was filled with fluid that would need to be drawn out and examined. The fluid would be sent for culture, examined under the microscope, checked for gout and bacteria, and finally sent to the lab and saved in case other tests became necessary later in his treatment.

At this hour, there were no technical support people in the hospital, and these procedures, and all transport, were my responsibility. It would be necessary to get the results back from his basic blood tests and knee fluid examination to confirm the presumptive diagnosis of an infected knee. If Eddie's knee *was* infected, then there would also be a trip to the pharmacy to get the antibiotics, start an IV, mix the antibiotics, and hang them.

The nausea from struggling out of deep sleep was easing. I resigned myself to four hours of intense work and set to it. The hardest part of these midnight admissions was always the first steps.

My assumption was that because of his severe pain and high fever Eddie would not question the need to come into the hospital. In fact, this had never really been made explicit to him, although it always seemed clear to me.

"We need to numb your knee and drain off the fluid in it that's causing all that swelling," I said preparing him for what was to come. A few minutes later, I approached with a handful of sterilizing swabs, syringes, and tubes.

"Will it get rid of this pain, take some of this pain away, Doc?" Eddie inquired.

"There's a lot of pressure on the joint from all the swelling. Draining the knee will help some. You'll need to come into the hospital. It looks like the knee's infected, and if so, you're going to need a few days of antibiotic treatment run in through your veins."

"Wait, wait! You mean I have to stay in here?"

I played through my explanation again, in my zeal probably giving too much information. But I didn't anticipate his response.

"You can take out some water from my knee if that'll make me feel better. But I'm not staying here. I've got things I've got to do. Drain the water and I'm going," he said. "Give me some pills to take." And then, shaking his head vigorously for emphasis, he added, "I can't stay. No, I'm not staying in the hospital."

I had already learned that it was common for the people who lived around the University Hospital in one of the city's worst neighborhoods, to regard the hospital and doctors with distrust. Rumors of experimentation, of operations that patients never wanted or really understood, were common in the community. Still, it was a shock to me to have my intent and judgment questioned. *How could Eddie not see the obvious medical need?*

But the real issue had nothing to do with me. It was *him*! If his knee were infected, he could go downhill quickly. The infection could easily spread to his blood or extend to his brain or heart valves. And the knee itself would at the very least, be chewed up by the infection. Most likely he'd never walk right again. *This is bad*, I thought. *This guy can't just* walk out!

I explained the situation yet again. Then I explained it a third time. I suspected that the real issue was, it would soon be time for another fix, and Eddie wanted to get back out on the street. He also had distrust of the system. But that kind of delay was only going to let things get worse, and chances were that if he left, he might not make it back to the hospital at all.

I promised Eddie that we'd keep him comfortable. I asked him point blank about the drug thing if he needed to be out on the street again. I'd get him some methadone, to keep him controlled. The best I could get was a head shake, and "No, Doc, I understand. But I gotta go. I can't stay. I got stuff to do. I gotta get back out there."

He was a young guy. It didn't matter whether he was an addict or not – he was setting himself up to be disabled or die. He just *had* to understand. And time was passing. It was getting later, and we weren't getting any closer to getting him worked up, starting treatment, and getting him tucked in for the night.

Somewhere in the midst of all this, someone called my name. I looked up to see Dave, the chief resident. I didn't know how long he had been there. He hung out at the hospital at all hours of the day and night. His visits were usually an annoyance, since Dave felt honor-bound to find a shortcoming in *any* intern's work. He would bore into the chart of the patient you were evaluating, examining it page by page. Then he'd come up with a laundry list of things that he wanted corrected, immediately. It was never clear why he elected to prowl the hospital at these weird hours. *If I were chief*, I thought, *I'd be home asleep, not pontificating or trying to prove my academic macho to a tired and harried intern*. But I had come up with a great diversionary tactic that I often used to distract him. Dave was insecure about reading ECGs, while in fact I had grown skilled in their interpretation. Approaching Dave with a long ECG strip in hand and greeting him with a cheerful, "Hey Dave, can you help me look at this complicated ECG strip?" was usually enough to send him scurrying. *One-upped him again*.

But tonight, there hadn't been an opportunity to get

an ECG, so there wasn't even a remote chance of pulling off this ploy. There really hadn't even been much of a chance to get started, short of a tedious, futile attempt to persuade Eddie to get treated.

I looked up and realized Dave had been leaning against the wall, watching me, eavesdropping on the whole conversation.

Dave was laughing. "You're pretty funny," he offered. "Why don't you stop talking, let him go, and then you can get to bed." I stared at him in disbelief. I started to tell him about the patient, about the infected knee and the risk and outcomes and what could happen. He listened impatiently through a few sentences and then broke in.

"I know all that stuff," Dave countered. "I heard you say it all. But the man doesn't want to be admitted. It's not your fault. And if he comes in, you'll be up all night with him. And complaining tomorrow about how full your service is and how many patients you're carrying. You've already gotten credit for the admission, so you're back at the bottom of the list. It's 2:00 a.m. He's an addict, and he wants to get back out for a hit. Let him go and you can still get five hours of sleep."

"But Dave –" I started back again, but he interrupted.

"Fine, be a hero. I'll watch. It's a good debate and a great show." And he went over and leaned back up against the wall.

I turned back to Eddie and realized he had heard the

whole sidebar conversation with Dave. I had been so focused that I had totally forgotten that the patient was within earshot.

"Who is that guy?" Eddie asked.

I explained about the chief resident being the head administrative doc in charge of interns and the teaching program. I was tired now, growing weary and impatient, and a bit burned and belittled by Dave's comments. I mustered all the energy I had left. Then I started the conversation with Eddie again about coming into the hospital. I pushed and prodded.

Eddie seemed to think it over again. He looked back over at Dave and then he looked back at me.

"OK, Doc, so I get it. I see it now. Yah, I got it. I'll tell you what I'll do for you. I'll do you a favor. I'll do what you say. Go ahead: draw off this water from my knee and stuff. Get me a bed in here; get me a bed."

He turned back toward Dave, who was laughing again and now about to walk out the ER door.

"Hey! Hey, you," he yelled after him. "I'm coming in! I'm coming in!"

I turned and looked back at Eddie.

"That's good," I said, "that's the right decision. You're making the right choice," I repeated.

"Keep telling yourself that when you see the sun come up," Dave said laughing.

It was his last barb as he turned and started out the

ER doors. I refocused my attention back to Eddie. I was tired but relieved. Very relieved.

"You really made the right choice," I reiterated. "That knee infection is like a time bomb. All the redness, fluid, and swelling you have shown me that without antibiotics, the infection would spread through your whole body."

I paused and envisioned what the next few days might look like had Eddie left without treatment. As the infection took hold, he would get weaker. More organs would become involved. Maybe he would collapse somewhere out on the street. Even if he came to the ER again, the odds of his recovery would be slim. I thought too, that maybe Dave's sarcasm helped convince Eddie that I was telling the truth. I wasn't sure. In any case, I was glad that it had turned out as it had. I took a few minutes to savor my relief.

7

MEDICAL MENTOR

The senior physician came in quietly through a side entrance at the back of the auditorium. He was about fifty-five years old, heavyset with slightly thinning gray hair. Dr. Bill's entrance was hardly noticed as he sat down silently, slumping slightly in his chair in the last row of seats. Leaning back, he listened.

It was 10 a.m. on a Thursday, and the weekly clinical teaching conference was beginning. These weekly teaching rounds were well attended. They provided the opportunity to learn from the one or two challenging cases that were discussed during the hour-long meeting.

The intern who had been caring for the day's first patient began his presentation.

"The patient was an eighty-year-old white male who came to the Emergency Room with a two-week history at home of fevers as high as 102 degrees. During the two weeks the patient had been hospitalized, he experienced nightly temperature elevations without any obvious cause or focus." The intern went on to outline his observations, filling in details he thought most important.

"The patient was oriented, but frail and mildly dehydrated. His workup had included a normal chest X-ray, and negative cultures of his blood, sputum, and urine."

When the intern finished, the group began considering possible diagnoses and treatment plans. The discussion quickly became lively, as many of the doctors joined in and offered their diverse opinions. But the case remained puzzling, and despite much thoughtful input the group soon reached an impasse. At that point, as if on cue, everyone seemed to swivel in their seats and shift their attention to the attending physician who had been sitting quietly in the back row.

The attending leading the discussion shifted his attention to his colleague who sat quietly in the back. "What do you think, Bill?" he asked. "What would you do next?

Dr. Bill cleared his throat several times, furrowed his brow, and began to answer. His voice was deep and grave. He spoke slowly, enunciating each word carefully as if to emphasize its importance. His intense expression contributed to the air of gravitas that he projected.

"Well," he began, "we need to do things in proper order." He paused momentarily and cleared his throat another time. "The first thing I would do," he continued, "would be to take a very careful medical history and perform a thorough physical examination."

Early in my training I participated in teaching conferences with Dr. Bill. Over time, I heard him offer this comment on multiple occasions. I often wondered why this had been at the core of his response. Wasn't it obvious? After all, we had studied the proper way to take a history and perform a physical examination starting in the second year of medical school. We had studied the Blue Book, a primer on this subject, and made its content our own and practiced on hundreds of patients. It always felt disappointing to hear Dr. Bill say this. I had been hoping to learn some esoteric facts about rare and unusual diseases instead of receiving this simple admonition.

But one Friday during my internship, I sat down with another intern, Sam, so he could give me an update, as we were about to change services. He would be transferring his group of patients to my care.

"Do any of your patients have unusual problems or difficult issues?" I asked.

"There's one patient, Mrs. Winston, that we're having trouble with," Sam answered. "She's elderly and debilitated. She was admitted here from her home, where she had a series of caregivers. She had been spiking fevers nightly for almost four weeks. The family documented her temperatures at home before she was admitted. She has continued to spike nightly fevers since she's been here."

"I would expect your team has been actively working her up to determine the cause of her occult infection."

"Yes," Sam answered. "We asked the infectious disease team to see her in consultation a couple days ago. They are treating her as a fever of unknown origin (FUO). After they saw her, they ordered a repeat of lab tests and X-rays. The results didn't show any focus of infection or cause for her fevers. There doesn't seem to be an inflammation of her joints, her blood tests are basically normal, and there isn't any swelling or mass to suggest a malignancy; no swollen lymph glands or an abscess." An FUO was generally regarded as a clinical puzzle, the cause not determined for three or more weeks despite appropriate diagnostic efforts. I finished my conversation with Sam.

As soon as I could, I turned my attention to Mrs. Winston, the lady with the FUO. A review of her chart revealed that both at home and in the hospital, she had been almost completely bedridden. Although she responded to questions with short answers, it was unclear how accurate her responses were. The history obtained previously did not identify any occurrence that might have led to her current febrile state. Her daily fevers had begun without anything demonstrable having changed in her daily life.

Mrs. Winston spent most of her time in bed,

although her caregiver was able to transfer her from bed to a chair on most days. When she did succeed in getting into her chair, she did not find it comfortable and preferred to return to bed, lying on her back. The physical examination documented on her chart also was non-revealing. No one had found physical evidence of any pathology.

Remembering Dr. Bill's words, I started from the beginning. I had learned a mnemonic device that was supposed to be helpful in evaluating and locating a newly diagnosed fever. It went: "Wound, Wind, Walk, Water, Wectal."

This translated to: Wound – a surgical incision or area of recent surgery; Wind – a lung infection such as pneumonia or bronchitis; Walk – a blood clot in the leg or pelvis; Water – a urinary tract infection; and "Wectal" – a pelvic abscess, usually post-operative, found by performing a rectal examination.

Using this mnemonic device as a guide, I focused on ruling in or out any pathology. Although Mrs. Winston was frail, an examination guided by this approach came up negative. Then I went back to the protocol learned through the Blue Book, which meticulously outlined all the steps that constituted a "thorough physical examination." Even starting with "head, eyes, ears, and throat" and proceeding methodically through the book's outline, there was no identifiable source for Mrs. Winston's fever. *This is puzzling; what is going on here?*

After going down the list, I reached the final body organ system: her skin. Proceeding sequentially from her head to her feet, the front surface of her skin was intact and without any abnormalities. Finally, I had her roll over.

I stared in disbelief. *Unbelievable!*

Over Mrs. Winston's "tailbone," her sacrum, was an ulcerated bed sore about two inches across. This bedsore was totally obscured when she sat or lay on her back. Her FUO was suddenly no longer of UO!

* * *

After I finished training and had been in clinical practice a few years, I came to realize that Dr. Bill, crusty old doctor that he was, had indeed been an important mentor to me. I thought of his words often when faced with diagnostic challenges. Over time I appreciated more and more the simple truism that he had often repeated. "The first thing I would do is a take a complete medical history and perform a careful, thorough physical examination." As obvious as it seemed, it truly was a pearl of wisdom.

By chance, after I had been in clinical practice for a half-dozen years, I happened to meet Dr. Bill at a major national medical meeting. I greeted him enthusiastically, and we shook hands warmly. After we chatted awhile, I said, "Dr. Bill, I have thought of you often. I remembered how you would begin unraveling each teaching case with the admonition to 'take a careful medical history and perform a thorough physical examination.'" I paused. We both smiled with the recollection of these meetings.

I enjoyed having the chance to tell him about my experience with the lady who had an FUO from a "hidden" bedsore.

Dr. Bill smiled as I reached my conclusion. "Just as I said," he offered in the gravelly voice I remembered, "The first thing to do is to take a careful history and perform a thorough physical examination."

We shook hands again, smiled, and he walked slowly on his way. I had come to understand the gift he had given.

8

POLITICS OF NEW TECHNOLOGIES

My first assignment as an intern was on a dedicated cardiology service at the University of Chicago. About a month into this two-month rotation, my resident, Dr. Simon, paged me during morning rounds. She had just finished her internship and was beginning her first year in a supervisory role. I was the first intern she worked with in her new capacity.

"Jay," she said, "there's a fifty-five-year-old man, Mr. Nish, in the ER. He's had intermittent angina for the past two weeks. This morning, he had an episode lasting more than an hour. He finally decided to call 911 and was just brought to our ER."

"Do we have an ECG yet?"

"Yes, it's diagnostic of a major anterior heart attack. I

would like you to come to the ER and evaluate him. I'll meet you there."

Five minutes later, we met in the ER and reviewed Mr. Nish's situation. His ECG showed classic changes of an acute heart attack. Tracings taken from all points across his chest were markedly abnormal. Although his pain had diminished since his arrival in the ER, it was not entirely gone. He had been sweating during the more severe painful episodes and there were still small beads of perspiration on his forehead. I introduced myself and did a quick physical examination.

"As Dr. Simon told you," I explained, "we're going to admit you to the Coronary Care Unit so we can keep a close watch on you. It looks like you've had a significant heart attack and we want to be sure that the worst is behind you. I'll be taking you up to the CCU myself. After the nurses in the CCU finish checking your IVs and connecting you to the ECG monitor, we'll call your family so they can have a short visit with you."

I was to accompany Mr. Nish on his transfer from to the ER to the CCU for safety reasons. All patients with suspected or proven heart attacks were to have a doctor with them during transport so that any sudden, dangerous heart rhythm could immediately be treated.

As I prepared to leave, Dr. Simon stopped me. "Check his vital signs as soon as you get to the CCU. He may be very unstable."

Mr. Nish's transport to the CCU was uneventful. When we got there, his blood pressure was low and suggested early shock. His lungs had a few crackles reflecting early fluid accumulation, another finding suggestive of his fragile status.

In a few minutes Dr. Simon joined me again in the CCU. "Mr. Nish's condition is worrisome," I said. "His blood pressure is lower than I'd like to see. Do you think it would be a good idea to start him on an IV medicine to help his heartbeat more forcefully?" I half-asked, half-suggested. Dr. Simon agreed. After a short discussion, we decided on a plan. We would continue the medications already started. If the wet crackles in his lungs worsened, we would add a medicine to help clear the excess fluid. He would be monitored continuously in the CCU for any rhythm abnormalities. Over the next twelve to twenty-four hours his condition would, we hoped, stabilize, and allow us to wean him from the IV medicine.

Although we followed this plan, Mr. Nish remained unstable. While his condition did not deteriorate further, it also did not improve. On day four, Dr. Simon and I sat down to reassess our patient's situation. "Do you think he's made enough progress to try again to wean him off his IV heart medication?" I asked. "Or would it be a good idea to try?"

"It's time to try," Dr. Simon agreed, "but go slowly."

Over the next two days we tried to gradually reduce Mr. Nish's IV heart-strengthening medicine. But each time we slowed the infusion, his blood pressure fell. We were forced to hold off on any tapering. Even as he appeared to maintain the medical status quo, his condition was slowly deteriorating. The amount of supplemental oxygen he required to maintain oxygenation gradually increased. During the fourth night, his oxygen level decreased further, and his saturation started to fall.

By the next morning, it was clear that he needed additional support. A breathing tube was inserted, and he was put on a ventilator. The ventilator provided him with both a higher inhaled oxygen concentration and breathing support, both of which decreased the strain on his heart. With this intervention, his condition remained delicately balanced just short of a medical disaster.

In today's world, Mr. Nish would almost certainly have had a cardiac intervention on or soon after admission: an angiogram, likely followed by an angioplasty and stent or bypass surgery. These procedures are now performed in most major hospitals around the world, but this was not so in 1971. Coronary bypass surgery was new and not yet available at most hospitals; coronary angioplasty and stenting were not yet invented.

It was not until 1958 that a cardiologist at the Cleveland Clinic, Dr. Mason Sones, first conceived of a revolutionary method for taking X-ray pictures of the heart's individual coronary arteries. Serendipity played an important part in his finding.

Dr. Sones was using a long single catheter to inject X-ray dye into the aorta, the large, main artery carrying blood from the heart to the body. The catheter accidentally lodged in the opening of the right coronary artery, but before it could be repositioned, X-ray dye was injected selectively into the artery. The unanticipated result was a clear X-ray picture of the patient's individual right coronary artery. The patient tolerated this "mistake" without complications, and a new diagnostic tool was born. For the first time, this technology allowed correlation of blockages in the coronary arteries with angina, heart attacks, and heart failure.

Nearly a decade later, the Argentinian surgeon Rene Favaloro performed the first coronary bypass surgery at the Cleveland Clinic. He used a short length of vein from the patient's leg to sew a bypass graft for blood to flow around blocked or narrowed areas in the coronary artery.

I began my internship in 1971, only four years after this surgery was first performed. Many, if not most, hospitals, including the university hospital where Mr. Nish was hospitalized, did not yet have these therapeutic procedures in place.

Mr. Nish's clinical condition left me and Dr. Simon in a quandary. It was unclear how to proceed to best treat him. While he had not deteriorated further, he also was not improving.

We called our senior attending physician, Dr. Leon, for suggestions. Dr. Leon was a well-known and highly respected cardiologist in the greater Chicago area. Shortly thereafter, the three of us sat down to reassess Mr. Nish's condition and discuss the treatment options available.

Mr. Nish had been on IV heart medicine since admission, we explained. His blood pressure had been difficult to maintain, and he hadn't tolerated attempts to taper the IV drip. "I'd like to examine him," Dr. Leon said.

The exam did not yield any surprises. There were still moist crackles in the bases of both lungs. The heart sounds were normal. We reviewed Mr. Nish's ECG again with Dr. Leon, as well as his chest X-ray and laboratory blood tests. There was no evidence that the heart attack had caused any unexpected complications. The severity of the initial damage to his heart muscle had left it unable to pump sufficient blood to meet the body's needs.

"I think we're running out of options," Dr. Leon said. He paused for a moment, seemingly lost in thought. "I have a colleague at the Cook County Hospital who heads the team that has started doing the new surgical coronary artery bypass procedure (CABG). They're one of the few places in the city doing it. I'm going to speak with him and see if he thinks Mr. Nish may be a candidate for this operation. Let's talk again in an hour."

When we met again with Dr. Leon, he was upbeat.

"I spoke with my associate at the Cook County Hospital. His team has operated on several patients like Mr. Nish, and they have done well. They suspect that in addition to the heart muscle destroyed during the heart attack, there are significant bordering areas of muscle that are stunned, but viable. They hypothesize that reestablishing blood flow to these areas will allow the heart to regain some of its lost pumping capacity.

"We're in the process of setting up our program to do coronary angiograms here at the University – we've ordered the necessary X-ray equipment and several of our attendings are arranging to observe and learn the new techniques at another institution that has a program in place. Two of our cardiovascular surgeons are training in a similar manner. I hope we will be ready to treat our first patient in about two months. I think we need to have CABG surgery on standby because the patient is often unstable after the angiogram." He paused. "Radiology would like to be the central hub for these new angio procedures, but I strongly believe that they should be done in a department that is prepared to deal with any problems that may arise. I think patients are best served by having the program under cardiology."

Then he turned to me and said, "Let's go and speak

with Mr. Nish's family. I had the ward secretary call them earlier and ask them to come here. We need to explain the situation to them."

Mr. Nish's wife and eldest son were waiting outside his room. We moved to a private consultation room. Dr. Leon asked me to summarize Mr. Nish's situation for them, then he joined in the conversation.

"Mr. Nish has not recovered as we have been hoping," he said. "At the moment he's holding steady, but it's unclear how long he will continue to do so. The longer he stays like this, the greater his risk."

Dr. Leon went on to briefly explain the procedure of coronary bypass surgery. As he neared the end of his explanation he said, "The operation is quite new. Our University Hospital program is just starting. We have not yet done the operation here, but I have a colleague at Cook County Hospital who heads their heart surgical team. His team has had experience with several patients like your husband. I think your husband would be best served if we transferred him there to have his surgery."

Mrs. Nish and her son did not hesitate. She answered, "If you think that's the best option, then please go ahead. When would you do it?"

"They're able and prepared to operate this afternoon. Delay increases his risk. If you agree, we should transfer him as soon as possible."

We all went into Mr. Nish's room. Because he was on a ventilator, he was quite sedated. Nonetheless, we repeated our explanations to him, and he seemed to understand. His family stayed while the nurses prepared him to be moved. I began to arrange for the transfer. Dr. Leon called his colleague at Cook County Hospital so that the surgical team there could begin preparations for Mr. Nish's arrival.

Then Dr. Leon told me that I would be the one to accompany Mr. Nish in the ambulance during his transfer.

My feelings about this assignment were mixed. The trust being placed in me was both complimentary and frightening: being responsible for Mr. Nish's survival during the transfer was intimidating. That this responsibility was being placed squarely on my shoulders was also a vote of confidence. It was unlikely that he would have a spontaneous adverse cardiac event during the ambulance ride, but it was not impossible. Whatever happened, I would have to deal with it by myself. After a month as the CCU intern I had a greater store of experience to call on, but I would have felt more secure if there had been a second doctor to share the responsibility.

In preparation for the move, Mr. Nish's two IVs and breathing tube were carefully secured and reinforced with generous amounts of surgical tape. Attention to the breathing tube was especially critical: Mr. Nish was still ventilator-dependent. There was no mechanical ventilator in the ambulance. If the breathing tube was inadvertently dislodged during the ambulance ride, it would be disastrous. It was unlikely that he would be able to breathe adequately on his own. With the breathing tube in place, ventilation would be accomplished using an Ambu bag. This was a balloon-like bag connected to oxygen with a one-way valve. I would manually squeeze it about fifteen times a minute to push oxygen-rich air into Mr. Nish's lungs. This would substitute for both the ventilator and the patient's own breathing. He would also be connected to a cardiac monitor so that his heart rhythm could be continuously observed. Several syringes were filled with Lidocaine, an intravenous medication used to treat abnormal heart rhythms. These would be available on standby if needed.

While the preparations for Mr. Nish's transfer were going on, the chief of the radiology department walked up to wait for Dr. Leon. One of his staff had told him that a patient was being prepared for transfer to the Cook County Hospital to have a coronary angiogram. In a couple of minutes Dr. Leon came by to see how the transfer preparations were progressing.

In stark contrast to Dr. Leon, who was about five foot four and of slight build, the radiology chief was a very large, tall man. "I understand this patient is being transferred to Cook County Hospital to have a coronary angiogram," the radiology chief said to Dr. Leon, looming over him. "Why are you doing that? We've just installed X-ray equipment that could do this, and it sounds like your patient would be an ideal first candidate. We should do it here in our department."

Dr. Leon paused and then answered in a controlled voice, "As we have said in earlier discussions, these patients, and Mr. Nish in particular, are unstable. The angiogram is only one part of their diagnosis and treatment. A County surgical team will be ready if needed. This is the arrangement that is safest for the patient."

The radiology chief stared at Dr. Leon, who had already turned his attention back to Mr. Nish. "We've had these discussions before," Dr. Leon said to the assembled group.

With that, the chief walked slowly away. He made no further comments.

* * *

It took about an hour to make all the necessary arrangements. The family was given directions and left in anticipation of his arrival at Cook County Hospital. Once Mr. Nish was removed from the ventilator, I had to breathe for him by continuously squeezing his Ambu bag. I walked beside him from the CCU to the waiting ambulance, where his gurney and IVs were carefully secured. Then I climbed into the ambulance and sat next to him. I braced myself for what I expected would be a wild ride. It was 4:00 p.m. on a Friday in the summer in Chicago. We would be navigating expressways as fast as possible at the peak of rush hour.

Dr. Leon came down and we went through a mental checklist together.

"I think we're all set," he said.

"Does the Cook County Hospital surgical team know that we'll be there in less than thirty minutes?" I asked.

"I just spoke to the Cook County Hospital Surgical team again. They will meet you and Mr. Nish at the ER. An operating room is ready, and Mr. Nish will go there directly if needed once his angiogram is complete." He handed me copies of Mr. Nish's key medical records to give to the hospital team. These included ECGs, chest X-rays, and lab reports from the last five days.

The ambulance driver turned on his flashing red lights and siren. The doors were closed and suddenly my world became very small and focused. I sat by the head of the gurney and rhythmically squeezed the Ambu bag fourteen times a minute to breathe for Mr. Nish. *Hold steady, count, squeeze.....*

As expected, the ambulance drove as fast as possible. We moved around traffic, weaving from lane to lane.

Sometimes the driver sped along the shoulder as he attempted to bypass pockets of stopped traffic. It was a struggle to keep my balance and not pull dangerously on the patient's breathing tube. My focus on protecting Mr. Nish helped keep my mind off the collective risk we were taking as we tried to get to the County ER. By this time, the lack of medical backup was no longer an active concern.

I hung on, and thanks to our skillful driver, soon arrived at County.

The ambulance doors opened. The cardiology and surgical teams were waiting, and Mr. Nish was transferred directly on his gurney to the Cath Lab, while an OR was on standby. I didn't even get to give a status report to the waiting team. I didn't get a chance to wish Mr. Nish goodbye and good luck. I had spent a week caring for this very sick man: it seemed like the team was waiting for a new *case*, but I had just transferred my *patient*.

The ambulance driver turned to me and asked if I wanted a ride back to the University Hospital. If not for him, I would have had to get a cab.

About two weeks later, I learned that Mr. Nish had survived. Dr. Leon was kept updated through his colleague at the county hospital, and Mr. Nish had recovered fully from his coronary bypass operation. He was discharged home and walked out of the hospital unassisted. I never saw him again.

Over the next few years, struggles for political control of coronary angiography played out at most major institutions, but ultimately, coronary angiography (and later coronary angioplasty and stenting) became the domain of the cardiology department. These procedures are now used to interrupt an acute heart attack.

Cardiac bypass surgery remains available as needed. Today these procedures have become part of the "standard of care" available at virtually all major hospitals. The most important consideration is to assure that patient safety and technical competence remain the number one driver of these decisions.

PART III

CARDIOLOGY FELLOWSHIP, 1975–1977

9

PLAQUE-BUSTER PIONEERS

John Simpson got to the cath lab before I did. He looked up as I walked in. He was an imposing man, well over six feet tall. I had been told he was from Texas, and he spoke with a cheerful voice and a southern drawl. With a hint of a smile he asked, "Are you going to be my senior fellow for my first cath lab rotation?"

"Looks like it's you and me," I said. "Let's get started."

In many areas, medical training resembled an apprenticeship. This was especially true when we were learning to perform procedures, whether something as straightforward as drawing blood or starting IVs, or skills as complicated as surgical operations. Gaining proficiency in heart catheterizations followed this pattern. A senior, experienced cardiology fellow in their second and final year of training, partnered with a first-year trainee. They worked as a team, with the initiate gradually assuming increasing responsibility. In this case, although John and I had previously interacted casually, we had not yet worked together on a clinical service.

The heart catheterization was done as a sterile procedure. We each took off any watches and rings we were wearing and put on protective, X-ray shielding lead aprons. We donned surgical masks and then methodically scrubbed our fingers, hands, and forearms with a sterile brush embedded with bactericidal soap. The scrubbing protocol took over five minutes. After drying our hands with sterile towels, we each donned a traditional green surgical gown and put on our sterile gloves. At this point we were finally ready to begin the procedure. The patient had arrived thirty minutes earlier and lay quietly on the cath table as we made our preparations.

Using a sterilizing solution, John washed the patient's groin area which lay over the large (femoral) artery and vein. He scrubbed the area with iodine two times and draped it with a sterile sheet with a center opening. This would be the entry site for the catheters that would be gently passed retrograde through the inside of these blood vessels back into the heart. We then turned our attention to a small table beside us. This too was sterile territory. It held various supplies for the catheterization procedure such as needles, syringes, and

Lidocaine. The catheters we would be using for the procedure also lay on this table, each one coiled and sandwiched inside in a flat, sterile packet slightly larger than a sheet of standard typing paper. When extended, the catheters were about as long as the patient was tall, as their course during the procedure would take them from the groin inside the blood vessels to the upper chest and then into the heart itself.

What our eyes would see during the heart Cath, was the two-dimensional X-ray image of our catheter as we moved it through the chest's structures. Moving ahead, I turned to John and said, "We need to get the catheters out and flush them with sterile saline." He casually picked up a pack with its coiled, wrapped catheter and, appearing very relaxed, started to open it. I was not fully focused on him as he did this.

Suddenly, as if it were being liberated from a space too small, the catheter began to uncoil and snap from its wrapping. It threatened to straighten to its full length.

"John," I exclaimed with some alarm, "don't drop it on the floor!"

John looked over at me. He had never lost his hold on the catheter, even as it seemed ready to escape from his grip.

"Well, Jay," he said with a pronounced drawl and a grin that stretched from ear to ear, "of course I was *planning* to drop it on the floor!"

That episode remained a private joke between us, for

the remaining time we shared as Cardiology fellows and beyond. When we saw each other at national cardiology conferences, the recollection of that morning would always evoke a smile.

At the end of my two-year Cardiology fellowship at Stanford, I moved back to Chicago, my home city, where I joined a busy clinical practice at a large teaching hospital.

John stayed on at Stanford.

Like me, John had been present in the cardiology department conference at which Grüntzig presented his early work on balloon coronary angioplasty, abbreviated as PTCA. The abbreviation indicates that the procedure is done through the skin (percutaneously) repairing the inside (lumen) of the coronary artery by undergoing a "plasty" (repair). John too had been fascinated by the treatment possibilities that the new technique offered. He recognized, however, that the new angioplasty technique, although revolutionary, also had serious limitations and presented some challenges. On completion of his fellowship, John continued to work directing his efforts toward modifying and improving the first generation of angioplasty catheters.

There were two challenges that he addressed. To begin the procedure, a guiding catheter was introduced and advanced to the beginning of the target artery. The balloon catheter had to pass through normal areas of the target artery as it was advanced to the blockage. This balloon catheter was tipped with a short (one centimeter), very flexible guide wire. The balloon catheter itself, however, needed a certain amount of inherent "stiffness" to advance it through the guiding catheter and reach the target blockage. This was the first challenge.

The stiffer the balloon catheter, the more readily it could be advanced through the coronary vessels to reach target blockage, but the more likely it was to damage normal segments of the artery, even if advanced with great care. Competing needs presented an engineering paradox: obligatory stiffness conferred increasing risk.

There was also a second major challenge. The coronary arteries curved and branched, serpentine, as they coursed from their origin to the farther reaches of the heart muscle. It was frequently impossible to steer and advance the balloon catheter into a particular branch, or as far as needed to reach a distant blockage. There was not, at this time, any way to steer the catheter and make it "turn corners" when needed. John conceived a solution that simultaneously addressed both issues – the need to steer the catheter, and the risk of increasing stiffness. His solution was elegant in its relative simplicity.

John modified the balloon catheter to have a hollow shaft rather than a solid one. He then passed a guide wire through this central opening. In essence, he created a long miniature tube as the shaft of the balloon catheter. The guide wires were relatively stiff except at their farthest tip. They could move freely forward or backward through the opening that ran the length of the balloon catheter. The guide wire also could be rotated at will in either a clockwise or counterclockwise direction. Because of its relative stiffness, it imparted rotational motion all the way to its tip, where it exited the balloon catheter. The far end of the guide wire, however, was soft, flexible, and atraumatic. It could be bent to a curved configuration and retain this curvature as it advanced out the balloon catheter tip into the target artery. Rotating the guide wire as it was advanced allowed it to be steered. It could then be positioned on the target lesion with great success. By passing the balloon catheter over a guide wire that had previously been carefully placed, he created a safe route for the balloon catheter to follow.

If it was necessary to visualize the status of a dilated lesion, the wire could remain across the dilated lesion while the balloon was withdrawn. This allowed safe visualization of the treated blockage while ensuring that the lesion could be safely recrossed and further dilated if necessary. "Over the wire" technology was a major advance that soon became the standard for PTCA.

This is so brilliant in its simplicity, I thought. I could hardly wait to bring this new technique to my patients. John's invention changed the way cardiac care was delivered forever.

* * *

John, it turned out, had a brilliant creative and entrepreneurial mind. He saw opportunity in meeting challenges, and his innovations in catheter design radically broadened the reach of coronary balloon angioplasty. He made it suitable therapy for many more patients than previously had been candidates. His innovations led him, along with other Stanford associates, to form a new company, Advanced Cardiovascular Systems (ACS), which soon became a major source of cutting-edge angioplasty tools.

ACS, it turned out, was only the first of multiple companies John would start. He continued to invent new tools to enable the nonsurgical treatment of coronary artery disease. His biomedical engineering breakthroughs redefined what was possible using a catheter—he revolutionized the landscape for treatment of heart disease.

* * *

There was another cardiologist whose exceptional interventional skills extended boundaries of the "possible" with the new steerable PTCA catheters. Despite advances in balloon catheter design, it remained generally accepted that appropriate candidates for PTCA were patients with only one area of blockage needing treatment. Patients with blockages in multiple arteries, those with complete blockages, or those with complex lesions at points where the artery branched, were considered too complicated for PTCA.

This conventional wisdom was turned upside down by a brilliant cardiologist who radically expanded the indications for PTCA and redefined its limitations. Geoff Hartzler received his cardiology training at the Mayo Clinic. On the completion of his fellowship, he moved to Kansas City where he was a principal in the Mid-America Heart Institute. Geoff's genius exhibited itself in two areas. The first was his dexterity and unmatched skill in manipulating balloon catheters. He was able to correct blockages located virtually anywhere, in any branch of the coronary arteries. Lesions that had previously been considered unreachable were consistently reached, crossed, and dilated without difficulty. Geoff reasoned that if it was possible to treat single blockages with this apparent ease, why not dilate multiple lesions in more than one artery in a single heart? *How fortunate I was to be able to spend time with these innovators.*

Although Geoff pushed the envelope, he was in no way careless. He set a precedent that led to the gradual acceptance of multivessel PTCA. While it has now become routine, at the time Hartzler championed this approach, cardiac surgeons and many cardiologists were at best skeptical, if not frankly opposed. They thought

PTCA was dangerous and unproven. Many surgeons only reluctantly provided the required emergency stand-by for CABG.

A second treatment convention that Geoff disrupted led to another radical paradigm shift. It was accepted that heart catheterizations were not performed if a patient was having an acute heart attack. By chance, a patient of Geoff's who was scheduled for elective single vessel PTCA had the onset of a heart attack as he was about to be transported to the Cath lab. His diagnostic angiogram had been performed the day before, so his anatomy was known. Geoff decided to proceed with the PTCA despite the patient being in the process of an acute heart attack. He reasoned that this had been an accepted plan just a few minutes earlier and so should still be appropriate. In the Cath lab, he identified the blockage causing the heart attack, opened it with PTCA, and reestablished normal blood flow. The procedure was successful and uncomplicated. In addition, the marked weakness in the force of heart muscle contraction at the onset of the heart attack resolved. Muscle function had been preserved and returned to normal. Thus it was that Geoff upended two established, then-current conventions in cardiac care: he demonstrated the feasibility and benefit of complex multivessel PTCA, and he showed that PTCA could interrupt an acute heart attack and, in doing so, prevent muscle damage.

Geoff's work quickly became known among cardiologists working in the field. I had the opportunity to work with him at a time when PTCA's reach was expanding. A physician, Dr. Mel, came to me complaining of increasing exertional chest pain. Dr. Mel was an M.D. psychiatrist, and his internal medicine background was more than enough that he recognized his symptoms and probable diagnosis. I listened to his history and carefully performed his physical examination.

"Did I get it right?" Dr. Mel asked me. "Do you agree with my diagnosis?"

I agreed. "It sounds like you're having angina heart pain. We can evaluate you with an exercise treadmill stress test or follow our clinical intuition and go directly to coronary angiography. As you know, that will give us a clear answer with the least delay."

"Angiogram it is," Dr. Mel answered.

* * *

Several days later, his angiogram was complete. Although I had reviewed his films myself, I had him go with me to the viewing room adjacent to the cath lab so we could look at his angiogram together. The areas of blockage were obvious. There were several spots where the X-ray dye that outlined the inside of each artery narrowed to a thread. Of note, a tight narrowing was present in each of the three major arteries. Additionally, one artery had a short segment that was blocked completely.

I ran the films for Dr. Mel without saying anything. Although he likely had never viewed a coronary angiogram before, the areas of disease were obvious. Instead of the X-ray dye flowing in a smooth, winding tube of uniform diameter, the tube narrowed severely in the diseased areas, imparting an "hourglass" contour.

He looked at me with a troubled expression and said, "That doesn't look good, does it"?

"Looks like we've found the problem, although from the way you described your symptoms I'm not surprised."

"Where do we go from here?" Dr. Mel asked.

"Three vessel disease is considered an indication for coronary bypass surgery. The areas of your vessel narrowing are severe, at least 80 to 90 percent. One artery also has a segment that is totally occluded. With your symptom level and anatomy, I'd advise you not to delay."

"What about this new balloon angioplasty procedure?" Dr. Mel asked. "I read about it in the paper a week or two ago."

"Angioplasty is being done on patients who have a block in only one artery. That's the accepted indication. Maybe occasionally two arteries in the same patient are done, but that's unusual. I've done a few single vessel cases, but not anything with complex anatomy like you have. There are a few cardiologists performing PTCA on patients with several blockages, but that's not common or usual."

"I don't want to have open heart surgery if I can possibly avoid it," Dr. Mel said. "Can we get a second opinion?"

I agreed to make a couple of phone calls. I would have to send the films by Fed EX. In this era prior to digital imaging, cine film was the only media to document the angiogram. That afternoon I sent Dr. Mel's films to a University Hospital known as a leader in angioplasty treatment. A day later I received a call from the cardiology principal at the institution. He and his team had reviewed Dr. Mel's angiogram and discussed his case at length. They were unanimous in recommending that he have conventional bypass surgery rather than attempting PTCA in a case of his complexity. Dr. Mel was disappointed and unconvinced. If anything, the disappointment of this first "rejection" hardened his resolve to avoid surgery.

I had heard of Dr. Geoff Hartzler and his unconventional approach to PTCA. Somewhat in desperation, I called him that afternoon. I described Dr. Mel's coronary artery anatomy. "I have to be open with you," I said. "In the opinion of one prominent cardiovascular institution, PTCA was unlikely to be successful. They thought surgery was indicated."

"From your description, I can probably do him," Dr.

Hartzler offered. "But obviously I need to see his angiogram films before I can make a final decision."

The following morning, we sent Dr. Mel's angiogram films by FedEx to Dr. Hartzler at Mid-America Heart Institute in Kansas City. A day later, Hartzler called me.

"Jay," he began. "I can do Dr. Mel. Think of it like doing four or five patients needing single vessel PTCA except that they're all in the same patient. You need to move things along, so it doesn't take forever. The one artery that's completely blocked is more challenging, but I've done quite a few similar cases without problems. Why don't you bring Dr. Mel to us and come into the lab to watch the procedure?"

Dr. Mel could not have been happier with this news. He seemed to discount any risk associated with a complex PTCA and this bold, unconventional approach. Early the next Monday he was admitted to Hartzler's service at Mid-America Heart Institute for PTCA. Hartzler appeared relaxed and at ease, and we were soon on a first-name basis. While Dr. Mel was being readied for the procedure, Geoff and I reviewed his angiogram again.

"This and the completely blocked artery will present the most challenge," Geoff said as he pointed to the large left artery running down the front surface of the heart. "I'll approach them first. Once they're dilated, the remaining couple lesions, as I said, should be like doing a couple single vessel cases in succession."

I donned the obligatory protective lead apron to shield me from the X-rays. We scrubbed at the large sink outside the lab. Once in the cath lab, I stood where I could see both Geoff's hands as he operated, and the catheter's movements on the X-ray screen. In short order he began the case.

What followed was a virtuoso demonstration that could only be characterized as spectacular. With apparent ease—and nonstop commentary on what he was doing, and why—Geoff selectively engaged and crossed the target blockages with the guide wire. The dilating balloons then readily followed the paths secured by the guide wires. After each dilatation, short test injections of X-ray dye confirmed the resolution of the target lesions.

The complex angioplasty procedure was over in just under an hour. Every lesion had disappeared as if by magic, and the completely blocked artery was now wide open.

Dr. Mel spent the rest of the day resting in bed and was on a plane back to Chicago two days later. His subsequent course was unremarkable.

Geoff invited me to stay and watch three previously scheduled cases, an offer which I gladly accepted. By the end of the day, it was apparent that the artful performance witnessed on Dr. Mel's case was the rule, not the exception. During a break between cases, I asked Geoff, "With all the variety of complex, difficult cases that are referred to you, how do you decide which you will be able to do?" His answer was profound in its simplicity.

Geoff said, "You have to know what the equipment will do in your hands!"

Geoff's unparalleled technical skill also reminded me of a conversation I'd had with a well-known and outstanding cardiovascular surgeon in Chicago. He was referred a patient born with a complex inherited heart malformation that needed surgical repair. Rather than undertake the case himself, and despite his extensive expertise in this field, he referred the patient to Dr. Denton Cooley. I asked him why he had done so rather than doing the operation himself.

"Jay," he said. "There are several very capable and outstanding cardiovascular surgeons, myself included. But Denton Cooley is in a class by himself. He truly has no equal. More than once I've seen him successfully operate on cases that no other surgeon could do. His ability is unique and unmatched."

Geoff Hartzler had become the Denton Cooley of PTCA.

* * *

I continued to perform PTCAs in my Chicago practice, gradually including cases of increasing complexity. Geoff continued to teach and operate. He kept extending the boundaries of what was possible with PTCA until his untimely death from cancer in 2012.

Looking back, I can see more clearly how I was involved in a spectacular revolution in cardiac care. Less than a decade after Grüntzig performed his first human PTCA, John Simpson invented steerable balloon catheters and Geoff Hartzler showed that these could be navigated to the far reaches of the coronary arteries to prevent or abort heart attacks.

Today, PTCA is often taken for granted and has come to be the standard of care. For example, just a few days ago, my roofing contractor was at our home assessing possible leaks.

"How have you been, Tom?"

"Oh," he began. "Not bad, but I had a couple stents put in a few weeks ago."

"What happened?" I asked. Tom didn't know that I was a retired cardiologist.

"I was having some chest heaviness. My primary care physician thought it was probably gas. It was getting bad, so he ordered a stress test with ultrasound. When they saw the results, they admitted me directly. I had PTCA with stenting the next day and went home the morning after."

"How have you been doing?" I asked in follow-up.

"No problem. I'm glad they could use the balloon instead of having to do open-heart bypass surgery. I recovered in no time at all."

Stories like this have become commonplace since the angioplasty revolution.

I continue to be grateful for the privilege of learning from these giants, and for being able to bring this knowledge into my own practice. Nothing could be more gratifying than intervening to impact a patient's life for the better, or to save that life with the PTCA tools available because of the genius of these pioneers and those who worked beside them.

10

KNOT WHAT WE EXPECTED

"You have to know what the equipment will do in your hands."

— GEOFFREY HARTZLER, M.D.

It was far from the outcome I had envisioned.

Three months into my Cardiology Fellowship, I would finally do my first heart catheterization. Somehow, I had come to regard this procedure as the moment when I would finally become a *real* cardiologist.

The technique was relatively straightforward. It required that I make a small incision in the patient's arm, and surgically isolate a segment of a vein—typically, the large vein coursing from the forearm to the upper arm in a path that took it over the elbow. Then I would introduce a hollow catheter tube into the vein, following its course with X-ray. With gentle pressure, the catheter would be advanced through successively larger areas of the vein in a path that led to the heart itself. The first heart chamber the catheter entered would be the right atrium. This was the reservoir where blood that had already delivered its oxygen to tissues throughout the body would collect momentarily, waiting. With the next heartbeat, this oxygen-poor blood would be pumped across the tricuspid, a valve so named because it comprised three leaflets. The tricuspid would fill the main right heart pumping chamber, the right ventricle, which would advance the blood to the lungs where it would be resupplied with new oxygen. A similar sequence ensued, with the freshly oxygenated blood collecting in the left heart chambers and pumped with each contraction to tissues throughout the body.

Today's (right) heart catheterization would measure the pressures inside the right heart's atrial and ventricular chambers. The pulmonary artery, which carried the blood to the lungs where its oxygen would be resupplied, would also have its pressure measured. These measurements were useful clinically to distinguish lung congestion due to heart failure from primary lung diseases.

I would be working with a second-year fellow, Dr. Sharon, with whom I shared an office cubicle. It was noteworthy that she had had an early interest in cardiac transplantation, which was, at the time, a new and growing area of clinical experience.

"Take a look at the catheter we'll be using," Dr. Sharon said. It was more than three feet long, which would allow it to reach the heart not only from the patient's arm but also from the femoral vein in the groin. It was made of a green, plastic-like material and was about an eighth of an inch in diameter. As I flushed the catheter with sterile saline, I commented to Dr. Sharon that it seemed remarkably soft and flexible.

"It's from an older material that isn't used in current catheters, particularly the catheters now used for coronary angiography. The newer catheters can transmit rotation from their insertion site all the way to their tip. This ability to rotate the tip of a catheter leftward or rightward from outside the body is necessary – it enables navigation of the valves and the internal curves around the inside of the heart."

Our conversation then turned to other cardiology matters, and we moved ahead to begin the case.

"Mr. Jones," I said. "We're going to wash the skin on the inside of your right arm with sterilizing solution and cover the rest of that area with sterile drapes. Do you have any last-minute questions before we start?"

"No, I think I'm set. Let's do it."

"I'm going to numb the area we washed and make a small incision so we can isolate your vein. You'll feel a pin-stick with the lidocaine, but it won't hurt after that."

The surgical isolation of the vein went smoothly. Dr. Sharon provided guidance and occasional assistance. I made a small skin cut, and with the help of a special tool introduced the catheter into the vein. As I advanced the catheter toward the heart the vein became larger. We recorded pressures from our entry site and, as the catheter approached, from the heart itself. It was a straightforward process to advance into the right atrium. This allowed the first pressure recording from inside the heart.

Up to this point, I had been advancing the catheter in nearly a straight line. But to pass the catheter from its initial entry site and into the right ventricular pumping chamber required it to turn and make a ninety-degree right-angle. I needed to torque and rotate the catheter at my end, advancing it as I did. *This is more difficult than I expected. Is something wrong?* I persisted in attempts to position the catheter further: through the pumping chamber and into the main pulmonary artery.

After about fifteen minutes of repeated but unsuccessful effort, Dr. Sharon and I agreed that we should conclude the procedure. We had collected a reasonable, if not complete, amount of pressure data. It was unlikely that further efforts to rotate or otherwise temporarily reconfigure the curvature of the catheter would be more successful.

It was time to remove the catheter and do the minor surgical repair of the arm entry site. With that, I slowly and carefully began to withdraw the catheter from Mr. Jones's arm. We anticipated finishing in ten or fifteen minutes.

After the catheter had been withdrawn about ten inches, there was sudden resistance. Withdrawal could not continue. A repeat X-ray of Mr. Jones's upper chest was surprising and alarming: the catheter had folded on itself and formed a loop. As it was withdrawn into the upper arm, the narrowing of the vein tightened the loop; attempting to push it forward now widened the loop. The catheter could neither be advanced nor withdrawn. It was stuck in place. *We're in deep trouble. How did we get into this mess?*

I looked at Dr. Sharon in disbelief, and then back at the X-ray. Our attempts to free the catheter by pushing, pulling, or twisting did nothing except, perhaps, lock the catheter more snugly in place. Our efforts to steer it and advance it further into the heart had not only been unsuccessful, but they had also been harmful.

I looked at Dr. Sharon again.

"Surgery?" I said, half a question and half a statement. We stepped away from the bedside, out of hearing range. The patient was groggy but still awake.

"Speak to Mr. Jones. I'll call the surgeon," she said.

It took me a few minutes to gather my thoughts. I knew that I had to balance honesty with an understanding of Mr. Jones's certain disappointment – and of my own.

Dr. Sharon walked to the nursing station to call, and I returned to Mr. Jones's bedside.

"Mr. Jones," I began, "We have a problem. The catheter twisted during your procedure. We're going to have to ask a surgeon to take it out. They'll make an incision in your arm so they can remove it. It has twisted on itself, creating a small knot. This is an unexpected problem. I'm sorry to have to give you this news."

He looked down, and then away.

"Is this something that happens often?" He asked.

"No, fortunately not."

"I'm sure you guys did your best. When will you do the surgery? Today?" He appeared resigned. *What a relief! The surgeon should be able to fix this. Not a good way to start.*

"Yes, today. Sooner rather than later. We don't want to leave the catheter in any longer than necessary." Dr. Sharon and I were both worried that clots might form in the vein around the knot.

Mr. Jones had surgery that same afternoon. He spent two more days in the hospital, and his post-op course was uneventful and uncomplicated. I visited him each of those days.

Dr. Sharon and I spoke about Mr. Jones several times. We did an in-depth case review. We decided that we had not appreciated the limitations of our equipment – the catheters, in this case. We had not understood how flexible they were and how poorly they transmitted rotation, particularly when they reached body temperature. Had we thought about this, our efforts to pass the catheter further into the heart would have been more restrained. The complication might have then been avoided. There is always a learning curve for new equipment and procedures. Today, there are simulation labs in most medical schools where practice can be done repeatedly to gain skill. This was not true fifty years ago.

Unfortunately, complications occur even with best efforts. It is helpful to have a general plan to deal with problems that arise. Every complication can be a learning experience. Re-evaluation of each problem with colleagues leads to better understanding of what went wrong and how to prevent reoccurrence. Most hospitals today have an M&M (Morbidity and Mortality) committee that meets on a regular basis to review all cases with unexpected outcomes; this is now a requirement for JCAH (Joint Commission for Accreditation of Hospitals) review and certification. The goal of the review is to identify problems or complications and to learn from them. This is particularly important in cases that involve use of new technologies or equipment. In this way, staff can continue to learn what the equipment will do in their hands and improve their skills.

"MY SON, THE DOCTOR!"

"How have you been feeling, Mom?" I asked during one of our weekly phone check-ups. "Are you still washing up with Dr. Shumway, honey?" she replied.

I must have told Mom about my Stanford cardiology fellowship at least three or four times already. There was no question about that, as proud as we both were, Mom was ambivalent. Why did I have to do my fellowship so far from Chicago where I grew up? Mom projected her feeling of loss as well as her pride.

Mom was of the first generation born in the U.S., and she had left the small Missouri city of her childhood in pursuit of an education. Yet she had difficulty accepting that my career decisions took me away from my hometown. Mom had a degree in Social Work from the University of Chicago. She was a poet, fluent in Hebrew, and a talented artist with a portfolio of still-life oil paintings as well as sculptures of a dozen small figures taken from stories like *Fiddler on the Roof*. With these accomplishments to her credit, her ambivalence about my career choice was perhaps peculiar, but she also felt lonely even before I left town. Occasionally, I overheard her say to her friends, "My son is a heart doctor." Maybe that helped her deal with her disappointment.

"Aren't there good programs here in Chicago? Do you really need to go all the way to *California*?"

In desperation I must have told her that Dr. Shumway was a world-famous heart surgeon, hoping this information would convince her that what I was doing made good sense. So far, I hadn't been successful.

When I paused, she repeated, "Honey, are you still washing up with that famous surgeon?"

"He washes up at home each morning before he comes to the hospital!" I told the joke without thinking.

Mom was puzzled. "But I thought he washed up before he did surgery."

"It's called 'scrubbing,' Mom. Not washing up. Dr. Shumway *scrubs* before he starts each operation."

"Isn't scrubbing the same as washing up?"

"Mom, everyone who will be close to the surgical area scrubs before they operate. Anyone touching the operation area must be super-clean. You don't want to cause an infection by getting germs into the body. Keeping things super-clean is very important. There's a ritual everyone must follow."

"Does Dr. Shumway scrub too, even if he's already washed up at home?"

Clearly, an explanation was in order. Mom's questions were charming to me, although sometimes a bit embarrassing. *How many of us are lucky enough to have an aging parent still wanting to keep up with their career?* I wondered.

I didn't remember what I had previously told her about Dr. Shumway. It was unlikely that I had ever described the ritual of surgical scrubbing. Filling in with a bit of history seemed to be a good idea. Here's what I told Mom:

Any procedure that cuts through the skin can bring germs or bacteria into the body. So to begin, everyone who will be involved puts on a mask. A nurse or operating room tech washes the area of the body that will be operated on with a sterilizing liquid. In addition to masks, the doctors and nurses wear sterile gloves. Next, they cover the skin around the area that's being operated with sterile towels so that only the exact area of interest stays uncovered. Now all the doctors, nurses and techs that will touch the sterilized area get ready for surgery.

Before they come into the OR, they change from their regular street clothes into scrub clothes, the green or light blue clothes you see medical people wearing in the hospital. To scrub, they wash their hands with a special little brush filled with sterilizing soap. Usually, they do this twice for a couple of minutes each time. The brush allows them to get to areas that are hard to reach, like under fingernails. Then they dry their hands with sterile towels. A nurse or tech helps them put on a surgical gown and their sterile gloves. Now they're ready to start. From now and for the rest of the operation they don't touch anything that is not sterile.

When I finished, Mom declared, "Now I understand!"

"It's quite a dance," I said. "After a while it becomes familiar, and you do it automatically."

"So, now tell me about this Dr. Shumway. Why is he famous? What about him is so special? Is he worth coming all the way out to California from Chicago just to see him?"

"He's a famous heart surgeon at Stanford Medical Center," I said. "He performed the first heart transplantation ever done in the United States, and the second ever done in the world."

"Why are you spending time working with him? I thought you were training to be a cardiologist, not a surgeon." It was clear that her interest had been aroused.

"A general cardiologist takes care of patients with

most conditions affecting the heart, except those requiring specific catheter procedures. These are done by interventional cardiologists. They do both medical heart care and tests using catheters. I'm learning cardiology interventions as part of my training."

"How many types of cardiologists are there? How am I supposed to explain this to my friends?"

"Just say that your son treats heart disease. I'm not sure all the detail makes it easier to understand, especially the first few times it's explained to them."

"Well, I want to understand. Tell me more about these different kinds of heart docs. I've heard some of it before." Mom was definitely trying to understand. If she could brag about me to her friends, that would make her disappointment at my choice more palatable. She could identify with my wanting the best education and experience. It seemed to appeal to her, especially when I compared surgery to her painting and sculpting. These were talents she identified with, and the parallels made sense to her.

"OK, Mom, here goes!"

"Interventional cardiologists do angiograms to demonstrate the arteries that give blood to the heart. These can show blockages that cause heart attacks. They make the road map that guides a heart surgeon doing a bypass operation. We work as a team with heart surgeons. The more a cardiologist understands the surgical aspects of heart care, including surgery itself, the better equipped they are to care for their patients."

"So, do you do heart surgery when you're with Dr. Shumway?"

"I watch, help, and care for the surgical patients before and after their operations. I do a lot of listening. I'm there to observe and to learn. Sometimes I hold instruments or trim sutures. Most of all, being in the operating room lets me see decisions as they are made. I see things as they happen in real time. It's an incredible opportunity to learn. I have the privilege of working with the best right now. It will prepare me to better care for my patients and share first-hand information with them. Preparation for an operation usually begins with the patient arriving in the OR about 6:30 a.m. The actual operation typically starts at around 7:30 a.m. and takes three or more hours. On most days a second operation starts around lunchtime. You're there by 6:30 a.m. every morning – you never know when something will happen and you'll have the chance to learn something critically important, something that may someday save a life. That's a lesson learned during internship: critical events happen when they happen. They don't follow any predictable schedule."

"So tell me, what makes Dr. Shumway so special?" Mom asked. *Is Mom just getting old or is her memory failing? She has asked this question before.*

"As I've said, Dr. Shumway did the first heart transplant in the United States. Shumway is methodical, and every motion of his hands is purposeful, precise. There is a rhythm and efficiency to each move. At first it appears to the uninitiated observer that he is moving quite slowly, but that isn't so."

"What kinds of operations have you seen recently?"

"A couple days ago Dr. Shumway replaced an aortic valve on a man who was born with his valve already narrowed and diseased. The narrowing was making his heart pump against abnormal resistance. The heart was starting to show signs of weakening. If not treated, the pumping chamber would continue to enlarge and wear out. He was at risk for heart failure at a very young age."

"That sounds interesting and important. I'm impressed." It was impossible not to smile. "Go on. Tell me about it," she said.

It was something beautiful to watch. Dr. Shumway made it look easy. It, in fact looked so straightforward that for a moment I almost felt like I could do it, which was of course ridiculous. He opened the chest from the front to gain access to the heart. The patient was connected to the heart-lung machine to keep his blood enriched with oxygen while the heart was stopped. The diseased valve was then carefully cut out to relieve the blockage. What was amazing was to see the replacement valve sewn in place. It was like watching an artist at work.

The valve itself is mounted on a circular metal ring.

Some valves are made from pig hearts and others are entirely of synthetic metal and plastic. Dr. Shumway sewed fine suture threads from the valve to the heart and back to the valve again. Both ends of each suture were held temporarily with a hemostat clamp. He placed these evenly all around the circular perimeter of both the valve and the aorta. Finally, he slid the valve down these sutures and then tied each securely. These held the replacement valve firmly in place over the aorta.

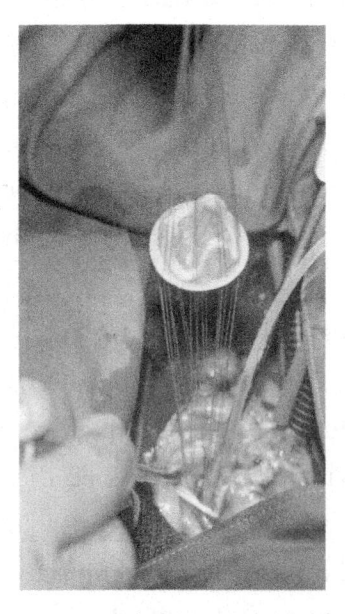

Open heart surgery showing insertion of artificial valve into human heart

"I've seen other heart surgeons do the valve replacement procedure. It wasn't the same. It just wasn't as smooth and graceful."

"Sounds exciting," Mom said. "Wait until I tell my friends that my son is doing surgery with a world-famous heart surgeon! Sounds like when I took courses with world-famous artist professors in graduate school."

Maybe Mom understands more clearly now. Maybe she won't feel so sad that I'm not in Chicago, I thought.

PART IV

PRIVATE PRACTICE, 1977–1998

"TRUST, BUT VERIFY"

My stepson Brian, who was fifty, had never seen my Thorens vinyl record player before. He looked at it carefully before commenting.

"This looks like it's from another era." He continued looking through the collection of records stacked neatly at the side. There was music by classical composers – Mozart and Beethoven and Brahms, and old classic discs of popular genres – and even an original Beatles album. Brian stopped shuffling through the stack. He held up a disc with a black jacket and a title printed on its front in bold red letters: *Listening to Heart Sounds*.

"What is this?"

"Just as it says," I answered, "it's a recording of the normal and abnormal heart sounds you can hear when you listen to the heart through a stethoscope. The record was recorded as a training tool, by a well-known cardiologist, Dr. Proctor Harvey, several years ago. It's a classic, a gem. Do you want to listen?" I asked.

He smiled and said with a chuckle, "Absolutely. I've got to hear this."

We put on the old record and started it playing. Dr. Harvey began to speak. His deep bass voice lent a serious air to his commentary. First, he presented the sound patterns associated with normal valve function. The sounds were generated by the closing of the tissue leaflets that formed the valve structures. These valves assured the one-way flow of blood through the heart's various chambers.

After explaining the sounds produced by normal valves, Dr. Harvey went on to methodically name various disease states and play the uniquely abnormal sounds associated with each. A leaking valve generated a distinct swishing sound with characteristic timing and pitch. A valve that was abnormally narrowed also generated abnormal swishing sounds, but with a different but typical pitch and timing. Thus, each of the four valves could generate its own unique sound pattern depending on whether it leaked or was narrowed. After we had listened to the record for a few minutes Brian looked incredulous.

"So, can you make heads or tails of that mix?" he asked. He was amazed when I affirmed that yes, I could.

"Brian," I said, "during my training I listened to

hundreds of hearts. Most were normal, but after you listen to many normal hearts, you begin to recognize abnormalities. And with more experience, you learn what the various abnormal patterns mean."

"Do docs still need to do that?" he asked. "I mean, with CAT scans and ultrasounds and MRIs, I would think that listening to those sounds with a stethoscope has become obsolete."

"Those are ways of taking pictures of the heart," I replied. "They have added immensely to our ability to make diagnoses, but there is still an important role for the stethoscope. It contributes important information to a patient's physical examination. It's a tool that you can always carry with you, literally in your pocket. You can't *image* every single patient. You need to have an idea what you're looking for. The stethoscope can be a tremendous help in figuring this out. The various sounds you hear make sense once you get familiar with what's going on.

"The heart is a pump, as you know. It has to keep the blood flowing through the lungs to get oxygen and then to the muscles and body organs that use that oxygen as fuel. The blood always needs to flow in a forward direction. The heart valves keep the blood from going backward.

"Normally that blood flow is smooth. Think of a river and the difference between white water and smooth, even flow. Turbulent flow makes noise. We call that noise a 'heart murmur.' When valves close normally, they also make characteristic sounds. With experience, a doc can tell by the location and timing of a heart murmur or valve closing sound, which valve is causing the turbulence and isn't working normally. It's not surprising. You play the guitar. You've learned to 'hear' mistakes, like a note that's out of tune or the wrong fingering of a chord.

"Let me tell you about a case I had shortly after I finished my Cardiology fellowship and started in practice. You'll see what I mean. It's one of many cases where the stethoscope played a very important role in patient care." We turned off the record player and sat down. "This case makes the point," I repeated in a dad-like way.

* * *

I had just started as a new Attending Physician in clinical practice with two other cardiologists. Early one afternoon, my senior partner paged to tell me that a young woman was being transferred to our care from another hospital. She had been diagnosed with a severely leaking heart valve in her aorta and was scheduled for open heart surgery the following morning to replace her diseased valve. We would be working with the Cardiac Surgeon to help care for her, particularly in the pre- and post-operative periods. She had undergone a diagnostic heart catheterization at the other hospital, and the data from this procedure would be brought to us later in the afternoon. It would include pictures taken while X-ray dye was injected through a small catheter tube positioned in her aorta just above the valve. This picture would document the severity of the leak that necessitated valve replacement.

About two hours after the call from my associate, the ward clerk paged me.

"Dr. K, your new patient, Sheila Jones, is here. The nurses have finished their admitting routine. You can see her whenever you're ready."

About a half hour later, I walked into Sheila's room on the medical ward. She was a young black woman who looked to be in her early thirties, of medium build and height – I mentally estimated her as being about five feet, seven inches and 130 lbs. A single mom who worked in a daycare center, she appeared somewhat anxious. Although she had been lying in bed, she immediately sat up and turned toward me as I walked in.

"Hi," I said. "I'm Dr. Kleiman, one of the doctors who'll be taking care of you while you're here at St. Joe's. I'm a heart specialist; a cardiologist. What's been going on that brought you to the hospital?"

"A couple of weeks ago I noticed that I was getting out of breath when I did my housework," Sheila began. "Vacuuming and the like. I'd had a cold a few weeks earlier and thought that was the reason. I went to my family doctor. He said he heard something abnormal when he listened to my heart. He sent me over to the Cook County Hospital to see a cardiologist. The County cardiologist did a heart catheter study on me, and said it showed a leaky heart valve in my aorta that needed surgery to replace it. I was sent here after my cath to have the surgery.

"This has been hard for me. It's far from my home and I don't have family or support here. This has all happened so fast. I'm very worried."

"I understand," I replied. "I'll have Social Services speak with you to see what help they can arrange. Let me ask you just a few more medical questions and examine you and then I will reach out to them.

"Have you ever been a patient in a hospital before?"

"Only to deliver my one baby. I haven't ever even needed to be on any medicines."

"Are you having any chest pain or shortness of breath, ankle swelling, or palpitations?"

"No, none. I felt well until this business started."

"Well, let me examine you now and take a listen to your heart," I said. "I'll start by having you lie down."

I held the stethoscope in my hands for a minute to warm the metal head. I had learned long ago that patients felt the head as cold and uncomfortable if I didn't do this.

I listened over the areas of Sheila's chest where heart valve sounds are generally best heard with Sheila on her back, on her left side, and sitting up, leaning forward with her breath blown out. Then I completed the remainder of her physical exam. Finally, I came back and listened again while doing all the maneuvers designed to bring the heart closer to the chest wall. These helped make any soft murmur easier to hear.

Sheila became anxious. "What did you hear?" she asked, her voice showing concern.

I smiled. "Let me finish and check things thoroughly. I'll go over it all fully with you, but I need to get a complete picture first."

I had been surprised by what I heard, or rather by what I *didn't* hear. The sounds of the valves opening and closing were completely normal. There was no heart murmur. I took a deep breath and listened one more time. Same thing.

* * *

I paused and looked at Brian.

"Bri," I said, "by that time in my career I had listened to hundreds of hearts. Most were normal, but still, a significant number had been abnormal. I knew what a leaking aortic valve would sound like."

* * *

I decided that there was nothing wrong with my ears! "Sheila, I'm not hearing anything abnormal. Your heart sounds perfectly OK to me. But it's important that I look at your cath and angiogram results and get the complete picture. I need to confirm my impression."

I left Sheila's room and walked over to the phone, picked it up, and called my senior associate.

"Steve," I said. "The new lady who came over for her aortic valve replacement tomorrow sounds totally normal. She doesn't have a trace of a murmur that I can make out. Can you get free and come over to take a listen?"

A short while later, Steve came over and I took him up to Sheila's room. "Sheila," I said. "This is my senior associate, Dr. Steve. He'd like to listen to your heart also."

Steve examined Sheila's heart. By this time, the extra attention was worrying her even more.

"Is something wrong?" she asked.

"Sheila, we aren't quite hearing what we expected," Steve said. "Don't worry. We'll get this sorted out and get back to you with some answers. We're getting the films from your heart cath from County later this afternoon. Once we've looked at them, we should know with certainty what's going on. Dr. Kleiman will be back in an hour or so."

Steve turned toward me, and we stepped out of the room.

"Jay," he said. "I agree with you. I hear only normal heart sounds, just as you said. The pictures from her heart catheterization are on the way – we'll look at them together to get resolution on this."

* * *

"Remember, Brian," I said. "This all happened before digital photography was even available. We had to wait for someone to bring us the canister of movie film taken of Sheila's heart during her earlier cath that day."

* * *

A short time later, we had Sheila's films in hand. Steve and I loaded them into the projector. We dimmed the lights and sat down to watch.

A catheter had been inserted into the aorta, allowing a bolus of X-ray dye to be injected into the aorta a few inches above the valve.

"The picture ought to show a lot of the injected dye flowing backward instead of forward across the aortic valve if she's got a big leak," I said, half to myself and half to Steve.

We watched expectantly.

"Look at the position of the catheter," I exclaimed. "It's way too close to the valve. Of course, it looks like the valve is failing."

The catheter used to inject X-ray dye was incorrectly positioned. It was literally sitting on top of the valve itself. A properly positioned catheter would have been sitting about three inches above the valve. There was indeed significant backflow of dye into the ventricle – but this had been caused by the forceful injection of dye with the catheter positioned so close to the valve that it pushed the dye backward through the pliable valve tissue. Sheila's valve was normal. The "leak" we saw on her cath was an artifact caused by human error.

"It's an artifact, not a real leak, isn't it?" I said.

Steve nodded his head in agreement.

I called the cardiac surgeon and introduced myself as the new doc on the heart team, telling him what we'd found so he could cancel Sheila's surgery.

"Dr. Steve and I have both examined Sheila Jones and reviewed her cath. Her cardiac exam is normal. It turns out that the catheter was sitting on top of the valve itself during the dye injection and the leak was an artifact. We listened to her heart and didn't hear any murmurs. We were initially puzzled but after reviewing her cath it all fit together. I'm going to explain the good news to her. She should be able to go home tonight or tomorrow morning."

"Thanks Jay. I'll call the operating room and have them take her off the morning schedule," the surgeon said.

I went back upstairs to see Sheila.

"Sheila, we've got good news for you. Your valve is normal. You do not need surgery. When they took the pictures during your cath, the catheter was too close to the valve. It was pretty much right on top of it. The dye is injected under pressure. With the catheter so close, dye shoots backward even with a normal valve. This made it look like there was a leak, when in fact there wasn't."

"Are you sure that there's no problem?" Sheila asked. "After all the rush, it's strange to totally change your recommendation."

"Yes, I understand, but all the parts of the puzzle fit together. Dr. Steve and I both found your exam to be normal." I had an idea. "Let me do this: I'll take you to the viewing room and show you your films. You don't need to be a doctor to understand what the cath showed. Later today, I'm also going to talk with your family doctor and sort out what he heard. Whatever it was, it was not caused by a leaking valve. We're all sure of that."

Sheila and I went to the cath lab viewing room. I explained what her films showed.

"I'm really surprised," Sheila said. It's easy to see how the flow is backward through the valve and the catheter is on top of the valve. Thank you."

"You can go home knowing that your heart is normal. I'm glad to be able to share the good news with you."

* * *

"So, Brian," I said. "Sheila did go home later that afternoon. It was a good ending."

"But why did you examine her when the primary doc, the County cardiologist, and the films all said she had a serious valve problem?"

"I didn't initially doubt the report or expect to be surprised," I answered. "I just wanted to correlate what I heard with my stethoscope with her cath report and the decision for surgery. Call it my own 'continuing education.' Valve surgery would have been a life-changing event for this young mom."

There's an old saying attributed to former president Reagan: "Trust, but verify."

13

BASED ON TRUST

I first met Shirley as a new consult. She had been admitted to the Coronary Care Unit (CCU) on the prior evening. I greeted her, introduced myself, and began to take her medical history. Shirley was seventy years old. She looked small in the big hospital bed.

"Good morning, Shirley. What brings you into the hospital today?" I asked.

"I was fine until about two or three weeks ago," she explained. "Then one day I noticed some chest pressure when I was carrying groceries into the house from my car. Over the past several weeks I've sometimes had the same feeling when I walk or do housework. It's coming more often now, and with less effort. Sometimes I feel out of breath when it happens."

* * *

In the late seventies, when I was a cardiology fellow at Stanford, one of our routine clinical conferences turned out to be anything but. An unexpected guest gave the presentation.

He began formally, and with great confidence. "Good day. I am Dr. Andreas Grüntzig from Zurich, Switzerland. Today I would like to share with you my work treating coronary heart disease, which I believe will change the way you practice."

Grüntzig's bold assertion, as well as his striking appearance, immediately captured our attention. He was an elegant looking man in his early forties, tall and thin with jet-black hair and a well-trimmed mustache. His voice was deep and resonant. His well-tailored, slim-cut suit contrasted with the casual California dress of the cardiology fellows and even their section chief.

There was a mounting sense of drama in the room as he continued. "I present to you my first patients," he said. "Each had a critical blockage in the beginning of a major heart artery documented on angiogram. Each also had an abnormal exercise stress test. All four patients were successfully treated by dilating their blockage with a small sausage shaped balloon tipped catheter. Following treatments, each patient's stress tests and angiogram became normal. I will present these results for the first time at next week's International Cardiology conference."

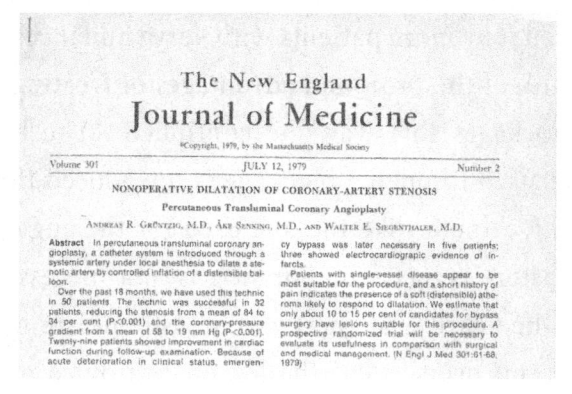

Medical journal article first describing coronary
balloon angioplasty (PTCA)

He paused, looked around the room, then dimmed the lights so we could see the angiogram films projected onto a big screen. Then he continued. "Here is the initial angiogram on the first patient. The artery is narrowed by 80 to 90 percent. The next picture was taken after balloon treatment."

A gasp broke the silence.

The residual narrowing was no more than 20 percent.

"When the balloon is inflated it pushes the fatty plaque, which is blocking the artery, against the blood vessel wall. In doing so, it 'opens' the artery and recreates a virtually normal path for the blood to flow. The treadmill done the day after the procedure was normal as well."

Grüntzig paused. A murmur filled the room. He then presented four more patients with very similar results.

"Think of the profound advantages of treating coronary blockages this way," he continued. "The balloon catheter used to open a blockage is introduced through a guiding catheter like the one used for the angiogram. No incision is needed. Surgery is not necessary to expose the heart! The chest and breastbone are not cut. There is no need to cut the leg to take out a piece of vein. The patient is awake and comfortable throughout. General anesthesia is not used! The recovery period is overnight, not a week or more. Think of what this could mean for patients."

While there was excitement in the room, there was also skepticism. Our cardiology chief stood up, dressed, as he sometimes was, in farmers' overalls with a button pinned to the bib front that read, "I'M THE CHIEF," and as he exited, we heard him say, "Aw, shit – this will never work!"

Grüntzig's enthusiasm was captivating. If other cardiologists could reproduce his results, they would revolutionize the treatment of coronary heart disease. From that moment on, I wanted to know more. This new procedure sparked my imagination. If patients learned about the new technique, they certainly would prefer it to open heart bypass surgery whenever possible.

The presentation generated intense widespread interest in Grüntzig's new balloon technique. In response, he started to give live teaching demonstrations to small groups of cardiologists at his home hospital in Switzerland.

Before long I was on a flight to Zurich, anxious to learn as much as possible at the hands of the master. I had anticipated this opportunity ever since Grüntzig's initial presentation at Stanford, and the demonstration course did not disappoint. He was a gifted teacher who graciously shared his experience of navigating the challenges and successes of his new technique.

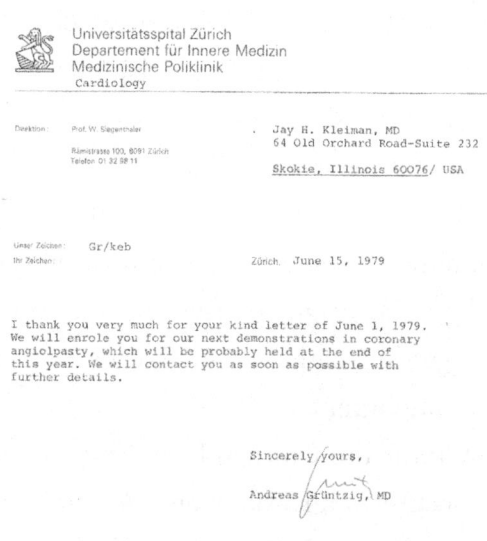

Letter from Grüntzig confirming my place in his heart angioplasty course

As is frequently the case, Grüntzig's innovation was made possible by the advances of many before him. For years, doctors had known that anginal chest pain and heart attacks were caused by the deposition of fatty debris called plaque that clogged the heart's coronary arteries. In the 1960s, doctors began visualizing the coronary arteries and their blockages by injecting X-ray dye directly into them. These arteries were narrow and curved multiple times as they coursed from their origin to the heart's apex. The arteries typically were about one eighth of an inch in diameter. As he demonstrated when he presented his early work at Stanford, Grüntzig sought to flatten the obstructing plaque against the vessel wall to reestablish normal blood flow.

Ultimately, he developed a narrow, flexible catheter with an inflatable sausage-shaped balloon at its tip. The beginning and tip of the balloon catheter were indicated by small metal markers visible on X-ray film. A soft, flexible guide wire at the front end of the balloon helped reduce trauma to the artery. The dilating balloon was advanced to the origin of the target coronary artery through a guiding catheter like that used for taking the diagnostic angiogram.

On my return to Chicago from Zurich, my first step was to secure approval from Administration and Department Chiefs. Next, I assembled an angioplasty team including surgeons and clinical support personnel.

Finally, I ordered the necessary catheters and balloons. Then it was time to find the first patient.

* * *

Grüntzig described appropriate patients as having a positive exercise stress test and a single blockage in a major heart artery. The blockage also needed to be close to the beginning of the involved artery so that the balloon-dilating catheter could readily reach it.

Several weeks passed without finding an appropriate patient. Then I was asked to see a new patient, Shirley, in consultation. Her clinical course and increasing angina suggested that she might be an excellent candidate for angiography and possible angioplasty. As it turned out, it would have been hard to imagine a more cooperative and trusting patient. The idea that she would be among the first patients to be treated with new technology captivated her – she relished the thought of being a pioneer. My enthusiasm seemed to kindle similar excitement in her. I tried to suppress my own anxiety. Shirley's trust in me encouraged me to forge ahead. I had been preparing for this day for months.

Shirley's description of chest pressure and breathlessness was not unusual.

"That sounds very typical for pain coming from blockages in the hearts arteries." I explained that it was angina, and happens to many people. As we get older, we often develop fatty deposits inside our heart's arteries. If these deposits accumulate and become severe, they may interfere with blood flow. The heart muscle becomes short of oxygen, and this leads to anginal chest pain.

The best test to assess her situation, I said, would be a coronary angiogram. "This test involves taking X-ray pictures of your heart's arteries. It sounds complicated, but it has become routine and is not at all painful. The area around the large artery in your leg is numbed, and then a small, hollow catheter tube is passed through the artery back to the heart. As unlikely as it sounds, you won't feel that at all! The tube is steered to the beginning of each of the heart's three major arteries and used to inject X-ray dye. The X-ray pictures let us clearly know if blocked arteries are causing your pain, and how best to treat it. The test takes about a half-hour to perform, and we will keep you comfortable, but awake.

"The alternative approach would be to record your electrocardiogram during progressively increasing exercise, a test known as a treadmill exercise stress test. If we were to do this, and it was normal, we would still have our doubts based on your history. But the definitive test, the angiogram, will give a clear answer." After some additional explanation, and discussion with her primary physician, Shirley was scheduled for the next morning.

Her angiogram confirmed our initial impression. The findings were dramatic. Of the three major arteries that nourished her heart, two were completely normal. There was, however, critical disease in Shirley's third artery, the left anterior descending (LAD). This artery was the largest of the three and the most important: it supplied blood to a major portion of her heart. It had a single, severe, 90 to 95 percent blockage in its beginning segment. Shirley's anatomy conformed to Grüntzig's criteria. If this artery were to close completely, Shirley would have a major, life-threatening heart attack. The severity of the narrowing suggested that the risk of closure in the near term was significant.

The timing of Shirley's hospitalization coincided with my practice's readiness to treat our first patient using PTCA. In addition to attending Grüntzig's course in Zurich, I had been in a colleague's cath lab and observed several PTCA procedures done by one of the few U.S. cardiologists who already had experience with the new technology.

Review of Shirley's films confirmed my initial impression. Her coronary anatomy was well suited to PTCA. Her severe single vessel blockage was sufficiently proximal to be reached by a balloon catheter.

I called her primary care physician to share my findings and discuss her treatment options. After giving him the background information, I told him that I wanted to suggest to Shirley that we treat her with PTCA. "We've already presented the necessary background information to the hospital's Ethical Review Committee and received their approval. We have their permission to proceed if Shirley is agreeable."

"Be sure you let her know that she would be your first patient to be treated this way," he said. "She may or may not be comfortable knowing this."

Late in the afternoon following Shirley's angiogram I circled back to her room. I intended to have a thorough discussion with her and would take whatever time was necessary to address all her questions and concerns. After checking that she was clinically stable following her procedure, I began.

"Shirley, we have clearly found your problem. One of your heart's main arteries has a very severe narrowing in its beginning portion. When you exercise or have physical or even emotional stress, your heart temporarily runs out of blood and oxygen. Fortunately, it doesn't look as if any permanent damage has occurred."

"Can you fix that, Doc?" she asked, "Before it closes completely, or I have a heart attack? Is there any medicine I can take? What should we do?"

"I think the artery is blocked enough to need repair. Medicine alone will not do this, but you have two treatment options. We can send you for heart bypass surgery. The surgeon will take a short piece of vein from your leg and sew a bypass around the blocked area in your artery. He will need to make incisions in both your leg and your chest. It's a big operation, but it's well established, and thousands are done every year with good success and low risk. Alternatively, we can use a new technique to repair your artery through a catheter like the one we used this morning to take your angiogram pictures."

I began to present the new PTCA option to her. The opportunity for Shirley to benefit if we used the new technique was significant. I briefly reviewed the history, rationale, and finally the mechanics of the angioplasty procedure, seeking to balance my enthusiasm and caution – I needed to tell her of the risk, as well as benefits.

"You would be the first person that we've treated in this way, and certainly one of the first, if not *the* first, in Chicago. A successful angioplasty procedure would avoid the need for bypass surgery. There is some risk though, that we wouldn't be able to get the artery open or keep it open. Currently, about one of three angioplasty cases are unsuccessful. The patient may then need surgery, sometimes as an emergency. We would have a surgical team on standby in the hospital in case you needed emergency surgery. Why don't you talk it over with your husband and write down your questions? I'll come by again this afternoon to talk to both of you." As I left the room, I breathed a heavy sigh. This would be new territory for both of us.

The cardiovascular surgeon was still in the hospital, having just transferred his day's first case from the OR to the ICU. He agreed to meet me in a few minutes to review Shirley's angiogram. The general attitude of cardiac surgeons toward coronary angioplasty was a mix of curiosity and tempered enthusiasm. Some thought outright that the procedure would not work, simply because it was new and had only been used on a relatively small number of patients. Others were skeptical for technical reasons. Some were cautiously optimistic that the new technique would make restoration of normal blood flow to "endangered" hearts possible for a greater number of patients.

Dr. Dave and I reviewed Shirley's angio films together. This would be his first exposure to the procedure, but from what I'd told him, he agreed that her clinical situation made her well suited. Her lesion was near the origin of the involved artery, it was clearly critical, and she was highly symptomatic. He arranged to meet with her later in the afternoon and explain his role should an emergency bypass be required.

Dr. Dave's buy-in was essential, not only so he could respond to emergencies but to facilitate general acceptance of the procedure among both patients and medical staff. Fortunately, we knew each other well. The coronary angiograms, which I frequently performed, served as the diagnostic road maps that were his guides in performing coronary bypass surgery. The import of his support could not be overestimated. His positive attitude contributed to my growing anticipation – we would finally be able to move ahead.

It had been just a month since I returned from Dr. Grüntzig's demonstration course, but the wait to find an appropriate patient for coronary angioplasty had seemed interminable. Now, it looked like the pieces were coming together and Shirley would benefit as we finally forged ahead. We had already ordered the balloons and catheters needed for the procedure. There was only one more arrangement to make.

I had been the sole observer of those three PTCA procedures done by a colleague, Dr. Gerald, at a nearby hospital in Milwaukee. That experience put me as close as possible to doing a PTCA without having hands-on, and Dr. Gerald volunteered to be present when we did our first several cases to offer any advice that might be useful. After a few more phone calls, the necessary coordination was in place.

Shirley was set to have her procedure as first case the following morning. The cath lab was scheduled; team members were confirmed. One, most critical, piece remained. It was time to circle back and to talk to Shirley, her husband, and any other family members with her. Particularly with a new procedure, it was obligatory that all the patient's questions be answered, and it was often helpful if one other person was present, typically a spouse or adult child. For legal purposes the patient must sign a consent form with a witness present to proceed. This is done before any sedation occurs. Shirley's husband was with her. He too appeared to be in his early seventies. He was not a large man, and his quiet manner complemented his wife's energy and enthusiasm. "How many of these procedures have you done, Doc?" he asked.

"This would be my first; I have observed eight. The first five were part of a clinical demonstration done by Dr. Grüntzig in Switzerland. He invented the procedure. He designed a new balloon catheter to treat blockages in the heart's arteries."

"Wait, did you say you went to Switzerland to learn the technique?" Shirley's husband asked. His surprise made it impossible for me not to smile. He was obviously impressed, and I was pleased and flattered by his excitement.

I discussed the possibility that the procedure could be unsuccessful and reassured Shirley's husband that the surgical team would be present on standby. "They'll be by to meet you later today. The advantage, and it's significant, is that with a successful PTCA you usually can go home the next day. The whole thing is done through a catheter inserted with just a needle stick like Shirley had earlier today. No surgical incisions are needed. The heart does not have to be exposed by opening the chest. There is no surgical wound, and she can get back to normal activity almost immediately."

I tried to present the pros and cons fairly, but my excitement and enthusiasm were intense. After several additional questions and some further discussion, both Shirley and her husband agreed to proceed with angioplasty as soon as the necessary arrangements were made.

Shirley was in the cath lab by 6:30 the next morning. She had been mildly sedated and appeared comfortable.

"Any last-minute questions?" I asked her as sterile drapes and various pieces of equipment were laid out.

"How long will this take?" she asked.

"Somewhere around two hours, depending on how long it takes to get the balloon correctly positioned in your artery and how readily the blockage responds to the balloon's pressure," I replied. "You'll be awake, but we'll keep you relaxed and comfortable."

There was an air of nervous excitement in the room, as well as a certain tension, when we began. The first part of the procedure was like the prior day's diagnostic angiogram. Shirley's groin was numbed with a small injection of Lidocaine. A guide catheter was placed in her leg artery and readily positioned in her left anterior descending artery, LAD, the artery with the blockage. Several pictures were taken to document her anatomy prior to PTCA.

The balloon angioplasty catheter was then passed through the guiding catheter into the target artery and positioned on the blockage. The presence of the balloon catheter on the narrowed, diseased part of the LAD further limited blood flow to the heart muscle. Almost immediately, Shirley's ECG began showing changes reflecting the shortage of blood flow past the site of blockage. In response, the nurse quickly increased the flow of oxygen through her nasal cannula. The room was quiet. The focus was intense and hyper alert.

We had entered new and unknown territory. No one knew how long her heart would tolerate being further deprived of blood and oxygen. Then, abnormal extra heartbeats began appearing in addition to the earlier ECG changes. The balloon's position was confirmed by the position of the small metal markers at its beginning and end. There was no way to improve blood flow other than to inflate or withdraw the balloon. "Inflate the balloon slowly. Gradually increase the pressure," I said to my assistant.

We all watched as the sausage-shaped balloon began to fill out. A narrowing persisted in its midportion, giving it the appearance of an hourglass turned on its side. "My chest is beginning to hurt," Shirley said. "This is like the pain I was having at home."

"The balloon is up," I answered. "Let us know if the pain gets worse." I looked across the room at the wall clock; the balloon had been up fifteen seconds. I decided to keep it inflated for thirty seconds. That seemed "reasonable," although we had little prior experience to guide us. My eyes moved quickly between the clock, the balloon's image on the X-ray monitor, and Shirley's ECG. Thirty seconds passed.

"Take the balloon down now." I waited a minute. "How's the pain?"

"Starting to go away," Shirley replied.

Her ECG began to normalize. A small test picture showed improved, but incomplete, resolution of the blockage.

"Shirley, we need to blow the balloon up again," I said. Then, addressing my assistant, "Bring the balloon up to six atmospheres for thirty seconds." The X-ray again showed the "hourglass" deformity in the balloon mid-portion, but the constraint was less than present originally. Fifteen seconds gave way to thirty. Shirley's ECG again showed changes reflecting the lack of oxygen. Her chest pain recurred, gradually increasing in intensity. Extra heartbeats emerged. A small dye test showed some further improvement. Although we were making progress, the LAD still showed significant residual blockage. It was "better," but still not optimal. We paused to allow Shirley's heart to rest for several minutes without blood flow interruption. Then we inflated the balloon for the third time. The balloon's configuration now showed significant further improvement. But suddenly, abnormal extra heartbeats emerged, hijacking the heart's rhythm with a continuous "run" of ventricular tachycardia, a dangerous and potentially life-threatening rhythm.

"Deflate the balloon," I said. I quickly pulled the collapsed balloon back from the lesion. It was no longer across the blocked segment, potentially interfering with the blood supply to the muscle beyond the blockage. The nurse had already started to move the emergency crash cart beside the X-ray table to ready it should it be needed to electrically shock the heart back to a normal rhythm. But the heart responded favorably to the improved blood flow when we pulled the balloon back from the narrowing. Almost immediately, Shirley's rhythm normalized. No further intervention was needed. Our collective tension eased a bit. The nurse relaxed her stance adjacent to the crash cart and started to inch it away from the X-ray table.

"How are you feeling?" I asked, in part at least to reassure myself that Shirley was back to her "normal."

"I had some pain and started to get dizzy, but that's gone now," she said. We took a collective deep breath. Another test dye injection showed that Shirley's artery was improved –better, but not fully normal. The original 90 to 95 percent blockage had been reduced to a 30 to 40 blockage. Markedly better, although still not normal. We were in a quandary.

A successful outcome with our first patient, even if not "perfect," would assure us that angioplasty could continue to be part of the expanding cardiovascular program. It would assure PTCA's potential to benefit other patients. Without a doubt, the improvement in

Shirley's artery was both obvious and dramatic. All eyes turned to me, awaiting a decision. It was my call. A huge weight landed on my shoulders. There wasn't the luxury of a long discussion, even if there were more experienced resource people to consult. There was no possibility of a call to Dr. Grüntzig in Zurich.

At this point in the world's experience with angioplasty, it wasn't known how Shirley's artery would heal. Would the residual narrowing resolve over time and become fully normal? Would it stay the same, or regress to a critical narrowing once again? The course of action that was best for Shirley was unknown. There was concern that repeat crossing of a blockage after withdrawing the balloon catheter could tear the artery, which could cause the artery to close abruptly. Doing additional inflations to further reduce the blockage might be ill advised or even catastrophic. It was decision time!

My process was straightforward. If we stopped now, her artery was significantly and obviously improved. The vessel might further repair itself during the healing process. I fought back the urge to do "better" and opted instead for patient safety.

"Shirley, we're done," I said. "Your artery is much better. There's still some small blockage left, so we'll have to see how it heals. But we've made definite progress. We'll keep you on heparin blood thinner overnight with a small, short catheter introducer in your leg and then take it out tomorrow morning. You'll have to stay in bed most of the day to let the leg artery seal off. If all goes well as expected, you can go home tomorrow night or the following morning. I'll be by to check on you a bit later. We can talk then about your follow-up plans."

Shirley did go home the next evening. As was the case with the patients that Grüntzig treated in his demonstration course, her follow-up stress test was normal.

Looking back, several important elements had come together: attendance at Grüntzig's conference; a trip to Switzerland to witness live demonstrations; stateside participation in additional cases; and a hospital that was ready to grow their Cardiology program. I was in the right place at the right time in my career.

The immediate issue had been finding a patient who needed an intervention and had the appropriate anatomy. Shirley was such a patient! The second issue was trust. Simply put, the patient had to decide to trust me. They would be meeting me for the first time. The patient was also being asked to trust my use of a new procedure which I would be performing on them for the first time. Shirley was anxious to proceed once she became aware that PTCA was minimally invasive and eliminated the trauma of an open-heart operation. She demonstrated enormous courage and a "leap of faith" in deciding to proceed. To her, the potential gain outweighed the associated risk.

Not all patients would have made that same decision. Many would rather have opted for the proven surgical approach. I had been quietly preparing for several years. My training and interventional skills, developed as a Fellow in Cardiology at Stanford, had prepared me. Cardiology was an exciting specialty where powerful new healing interventions were possible. I had the rare opportunity to be in the midst of a medical revolution. Who would have thought that a tiny sausage-shaped balloon could change medical history?

The safe and successful conclusion of Shirley's PTCA was met not only with celebration, but with quiet relief. It was a big win for her and her family. It was also a big win for our hospital and my practice. It assured us that while Shirley was the first, many more would follow. She and I were pioneers.

Heart patient says balloon treatment just swell

By Marcia Kramer

Just last week, Shirley Robins' arm was so numb from pain she couldn't comb her hair or brush her teeth.

Now, thanks to a relatively new technique, she's able to groom herself, and the source of her difficulty—severe chest pain caused by a narrowed heart artery—apparently has been corrected.

Robins, who said she feels "like brand new," attributed her recovery to "a miracle." Her doctors have a more scientific term for it: percutaneous transluminal coronary angioplasty, also known as a balloon catheterization procedure.

Until now, the two-year-old procedure has been used primarily in selected instances of hardening of the arteries in the leg.

Robins is believed to be the first patient in the Chicago area to undergo the procedure to remedy narrowed arteries around the heart, although it has been done elsewhere with encouraging results.

HER CARDIOLOGIST, Dr. Jay H. Kleiman, said he believes the technique may be applicable to as many as 10 percent of patients who, like Robins, otherwise might be candidates for coronary bypass surgery.

The catheterization technique and coronary artery bypass surgery take different approaches to attacking vein blockage that could result in a heart attack.

The bypass surgery, which was developed about 10 years ago and has grown in popularity, involves grafting a healthy blood vein, usually from a leg, as an alternative, or bypass, to a vein whose blood flow has been hampered by fatty cholesterol deposits.

The catheterization procedure attempts to restore normal blood flow to the blocked veins themselves through a technique that resembles inflating a toy balloon.

A catheter inserted into a blood vessel is lined up with the narrowed spot and then is inflated, like a balloon, to crush the fatty deposits against the sides of the vein.

PROPONENTS OF the catheterization procedure say it is less costly and less traumatic than surgery, mostly because the recuperation time is shorter.

But Kleiman was quick to note that "this is not, by any stretch of imagination, about to replace coronary bypass surgery."

At this point, the coronary catheterization is being limited to patients with severe chest pains caused by blockage in one of the three main blood vessels of the heart. In instances of two or three blocked blood vessels, as well as some cases of a single blocked blood vessel, the bypass surgery still is the recommended treatment.

In Robins' case, she was diagnosed as having angina pectoris, a severe chest pain that had spread to her arms, virtually immobilizing the 63-year-old resident of the West Rogers Park neighborhood.

A coronary angiogram, in which a dye discernible in X-rays is injected into the heart's blood vessels, revealed that one of the vessels was becoming choked off by fatty deposits.

On Friday in St. Joseph Hospital, under a local anesthesia, Robins underwent a catheterization procedure performed by Kleiman and Dr. Stanley J. Heller, director of the hospital's cardiovascular diagnostic laboratory. A surgical team was standing by but was not needed.

The procedure took two hours. About 24 hours later, Robins was combing her hair and brushing her teeth unassisted. She also walked unaided down the hospital's corridors.

She passed stress tests with flying colors, and a nuclear scan of her heart showed normal circulation. She'll remain on a blood thinner for several months after her release Thursday to try to deter further fatty deposits. Her outlook, said Kleiman, is "very good."

FEELING "like brand new," Shirley Robins recovers after undergoing procedure to remedy narrowed arteries around the heart. (Sun-Times Photo by Chuck Kirman)

First heart balloon angioplasty patient reported in a local Chicago newspaper

14

WALKING THE TIGHTROPE

His wife half-rose from her chair in expectation as I walked in, and the eyes of his family members fell on me in anticipation.

I forced a smile onto my face and said, "He's doing fine." I laughed a nervous, silent laugh and thought, *Thank God I don't have bad news to tell them all. That's a big family to have to face.* And then I remembered my little rhyme: "Everyone is someone's mother, father, brother, lover."

I was suddenly cold from the heavy sweat under my green scrubs. Sometimes, I think it's like going to war or being a cop in the worst part of town. You see the carnage, or the near misses and you try not to drown in them. If you didn't build walls, you couldn't keep going. But walls can also let the human side of you die, so you struggle to find the balance between caring and paralysis. The textbooks call this "detached concern." It's a tightrope you must constantly walk. Even so, you console yourself each time by realizing that you are skilled, and that the procedure needs to be done. The patient needs a clear diagnosis. But how do you explain that to a family suddenly drowning in a tsunami of worry, a family you may not have met before yesterday, or even this morning?

* * *

It began as a regular enough coronary angiogram. The patient was a fortyish young Black man with chest pain and an abnormal exercise treadmill test. The indication was solid. He had subjective symptoms. In addition, his abnormal stress test was objective evidence of a problem. Considering this, he was sent to have pictures taken of the arteries that supplied his heart; the coronary arteries that were keeping him alive. What was he going to do otherwise? If blockages in his coronary arteries went undetected, he risked suddenly dropping dead from a big heart attack. Or, at the other extreme, he could be burdened with the misdiagnosis of heart disease for the next thirty years. Maybe the abnormal treadmill stress test was a false positive and his arteries were totally normal. Maybe the pain was coming from his stomach or reflux into his esophagus. A wrong diagnosis could change his life, lead him to change his job, or worse yet, lose it; could lead him to take pills he did not need and might have a hard time paying for.

The angiogram would provide the definitive answer. So, it was reasonable; it was necessary to know. The question demanded an answer.

The patient had been transferred to the cardiac catheterization X-ray laboratory for his study a few minutes earlier. He was lightly sedated, but still able to speak and respond to directions. The femoral artery groin area was then numbed with a small injection of Lidocaine. The procedure went smoothly enough from a technical standpoint. The X-ray dyes now used were far less irritating to the heart then the ones used in early procedures. I placed the catheter in his femoral artery without any problem. The left coronary artery pictures were normal. Then I exchanged the left coronary catheter to the one used to take pictures of the right coronary artery.

No problems. I was moving along quickly, in the zone. Things become automatic and take on a rhythm that looks casual to someone seeing the procedure for the first time. But I was in the typical hyperalert, focused state, on the edge between tension and calm confidence, not expecting problems but always ready to deal with them. *OK settle down, you have been here before. The question needs to be answered.*

How many times had I done this? Hundreds – maybe

even more than a thousand. There was nothing that made today different from any other.

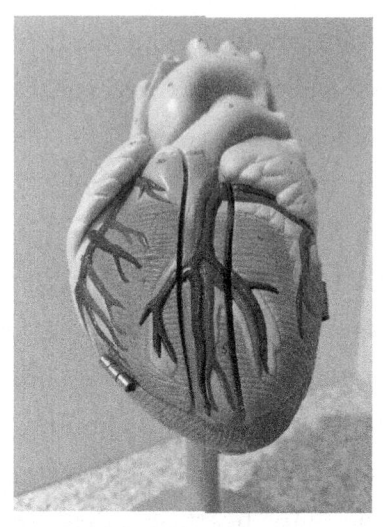

Model of the human heart

Having taken pictures of my patient's left coronary artery, I proceeded to prepare to visualize the right. I advanced the catheter, rotating it gradually. Then I saw it jump as it did when it entered the opening of the right coronary. I glanced up at the blood pressure measured through the catheter tip to make sure the tip was free and had not advanced too deeply into the artery where it could inadvertently obstruct flow.

The catheter was well positioned, so I moved ahead. It was standard to ask a patient to inhale when I took pictures, since this lowered their diaphragm and made the images much clearer. "Take in a deep breath and hold it," I began. There was a little bit of show in that. Somehow the sound of those phrases grew on me over the – years, and I liked the sing-song music of the chant. He looked at me and inhaled. "Hold it, deeper, deeper, *deeper* – and breathe."

I watched the X-ray dye fill the artery then flow down and through it. The vessel was large and smooth. The first picture was taken from a perspective looking over the patient's left shoulder to optimize visualization of the artery's curved, complex course. It looked normal so far. No blockages or fatty buildup.

"Take in another breath, deep breath – and *hold* it."

My left foot pressed the X-ray pedal. The size of the image was not large enough to visualize the path of the whole artery at once. The X-ray camera itself was fixed in a mount on the ceiling, while the heavy table where the patient lay moved on a ball bearing mechanism. And so I watched the dye flow down the artery and moved the table to track its course.

The second picture looked normal as well. I automatically glanced up at the pressure and ECG on the monitor. Everything still looked normal. *Well, good for him. One or two more pictures, and we'll be done.* It was almost time to relax. I was almost off the tightrope.

Once more now, I heard myself repeat the singsong, "Take a deep breath," followed by the sound of the X-ray film advancing. I saw the white dye on the screen flowing smoothly down the curving tube that was his right coronary artery.

His arteries were normal. *Good! A false positive!* Nonetheless, an important question had been answered. Now he would be home free.

I looked up one more time at the ECG monitor screen. The ECG trace was a sine wave, the ugly, undulating pattern of ventricular fibrillation (V-fib).

With ventricular fibrillation the heart quivers instead of beating rhythmically in a coordinated fashion. V-fib is totally chaotic. It is responsible for the sudden deaths you hear about where someone collapses without warning and falls to the ground dead. V-fib is a completely ineffective heart rhythm. It does not support any blood flow. In two to three minutes, brain damage sets in, unless CPR is effectively initiated.

I looked down for a split second and then back at the screen again. The undulating sine wave of V-fib was still there. There was an instant of denial, then an internal, silent curse and reality set in.

"He's fibrillating!" I called out. "Charge the paddles."

In the twenty to thirty seconds after the onset of V-fib, the patient starts to lose consciousness and his skin color fades. It's strange. I've been there many times before, yet it still feels unreal. Time stops. The focus in the room is intense, laser-like. Then, controlled chaos sets in.

The X-ray tower, fixed in the ceiling mount above

the table, prevented moving the defibrillating equipment into position over the patient. My right hand reached for and then found the table release button. I rotated the patient and table a quarter turn away from the tower, allowing access to his chest.

The nurse had rolled the emergency cart to the bedside and hit the charge button to activate the defibrillator. It made a high-pitched whine as it charged. Then the red ready light came on indicating that the defibrillator was charged and ready to use. It felt as if an eternity had passed. In the interim, I had been telling the patient to cough. The sudden pressure increase in his chest each time he coughed pumped a little bit of blood through the body. But now, as the V-fib persisted, he started to lose consciousness. I waited.

Early in my career, I defibrillated patients as quickly as I could. Ironically, if the doc moved too fast, the patient hadn't lost consciousness when they were defibrillated. They felt the jolt of the high-voltage electric shock. It hurt and they were sometimes angry and confused as they awoke.

So now I waited, taking another eternity of ten or fifteen seconds to spread electrical conducting jelly on both paddle surfaces. This prevented skin burns and assured optimal energy transfer.

The patient's eyes had now rolled back. The nurse turned his head to the side and readied the suction. She was prepared to aspirate any material if he vomited.

Around forty-five seconds had passed since the onset of V-fib. The patient had been unconscious for about ten seconds. I ordered the machine to be set to discharge energy in the intermediate range of 200 joules. One paddle was placed on the front of his chest over the sternum, and the other on his left side. I pressed firmly. "Everyone clear!" This warned the staff to avoid touching the table or patient and inadvertently being shocked themselves.

There is a red button on top of each paddle. To defibrillate the patient, they must both be pressed at the same time. This is a safety measure added to prevent discharging the machine unintentionally.

I pressed both. There was an instant's delay, and then the discharge. The patient jerked as the electrical current coursed through not only his heart, but his chest and arm muscles.

I looked up at the screen. The ECG was flat. Not unusual for the first few seconds after defibrillating. But then the ugly sine wave of V-fib emerged, not the normal and regular sinus heart rhythm that would restore life and function.

"Recharge! Clear!" Once again, I discharged the paddles, only to see that the same ugly sine wave reappear. More than a minute had passed. There was concern and tension in the room. Not panic, but concern.

* * *

I remembered for an instant flying out of Los Angeles from a meeting of the College of Cardiology. Three minutes after we lifted off there was a loud explosion. Then the plane banked steeply and started to turn. I happened to be sitting next to a young man who identified himself as a Navy pilot.

"We should be fine," he sought to reassure me and my wife Georgi. "We blew an engine, but a good pilot should be able to land OK with only one. We practice this all the time."

Then the airline pilot came on the P.A. to tell us that we had had some "mechanical difficulty" and were heading back to LAX.

* * *

"Recharge at 360 joules," I instructed, increasing the discharge energy. If this attempt at defibrillation was not successful, we would need to begin CPR. If we waited too long without maintaining oxygenation and circulation, the patient risked brain damage. His body lurched with the higher-current shock. I looked up at the ECG monitor. I was never aware of praying during these episodes, but when I saw his normal sinus rhythm reappear on the screen, I became aware that I was drenched in sweat.

Now, on the monitor, the blood pressure began to climb. Then our patient opened his eyes. He moaned and started to roll over. I held his legs so the catheter would not be pulled out accidentally. He slowly became alert and soon was mentally clear enough again to understand.

"You had a little irregularity of your heartbeat," I explained. "We had to straighten it out with a small electric shock, but you're fine. We'll be done in a minute." Fortunately, the loss of consciousness had kept the patient from feeling any pain and left him amnesiac about the event.

One more picture to go. I changed catheters again to one called a "pigtail" because of its curly-Q configuration. It's used to inject dye into the heart's main pumping chamber to assess the heart's strength. It might seem strange to continue and finish the procedure, but the information was necessary, and there was not an increased risk in concluding it. In this case, the V-fib was like an electrical accident and was unlikely to recur now that normalcy had been reestablished.

His angiogram was more than necessary, I thought. Consider the lives changed, lives saved. This patient was lucky to be normal, but the information might otherwise have saved his life.

His exercise stress test had been misleading. It had been a false positive, suggesting disease where there was none. False positive stress tests occurred in a small but still significant number of patients, maybe 10 to 15 percent.

I took off my surgical gown and heard a comforting snap as I pulled the gloves off my hands. I hung the heavy lead apron that shielded me from my daily exposure to X-rays on the rack on the wall. As I left the cardiac catheterization lab for the waiting room, my green scrubs were sweat wet. In the afternoon, once his sedation had worn off and after I had reviewed his films again, I would share the good news with him, his wife, and his family. He could continue all his normal activities. There was no need for new limitations. His heart's arteries were normal. I walked out of the lab to find his wife. She rose from her chair in anticipation as I approached her.

"He's doing fine," I said. "We're finished."

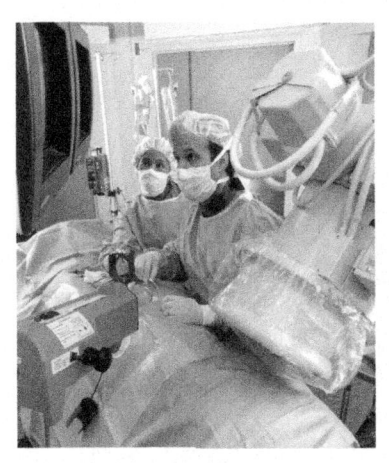

Heart catheterization laboratory for angiograms and PTCA, circa 1980

CHALLENGES

A bead of sweat ran down my back. Worried, aware again of the weight of the protective lead apron, I refocused.

The metronome-like cadence of Joe's heartbeat accelerated. The light pencil tracing his electrocardiogram started to rise at the end of each beat. Subtle at first, this part of his ECG coved upward more dramatically as the heart was further deprived of blood and oxygen. The heart rate continued to increase. It had been thirty minutes since I started the case – at that point, it seemed like yesterday.

There's a sweet rhythm to a case that goes well. The catheterization laboratory is set up the same way each time. Things are in their places – the same places. Hands find tools without looking, without steps. The body pivots; the hand extends, finds what is needed, then rotates back to the patient.

The patient lay on his back on a padded X-ray table waiting expectantly.

It was easy to find the syringe filled with Lidocaine.

"I'm going to give you some medicine to numb your groin, Joe," I said as I prepared to administer the Lidocaine as local anesthesia. "You'll feel a little stick, and it will burn for a few seconds. After that, you shouldn't feel anything painful, just some light touch and mild pressure, but nothing that hurts."

I probed for his femoral pulse. Then there was a needle stick and some burning as the groin area around the artery became numb. After twenty years, it was easy to find the femoral artery's pounding as Joe's pulse pushed back against my probing fingers. The needle stick was accurate, and a bright red jet of arterial blood spurted back. In seconds the catheter was gliding smoothly toward the heart.

"How are you doing now, Joe?"

"I felt some brief stinging, but nothing else. Have you started yet?"

Local anesthetic was truly miraculous!

"We'll be starting to take pictures in just a few seconds. It's going fine." My weight shifted as my right foot found the X-ray pedal. The lights dimmed. Then, addressing Joe once again, "Take a deep breath and hold it."

The X-ray film made its own characteristic sound as it advanced, a form of coarse machinery music. On the monitor, white X-ray dye outlined the heart's arteries as it flowed through the snake-like blood vessels and down the twisting, beating heart.

Thirty minutes prior, the stream of dye in Joe's principal left artery abruptly formed an hourglass, outlining a severe blockage. This blockage was critical, since it threatened to close a major artery that supplied blood to a large portion of his heart.

To the layman, this is the widow-maker.

But that was in the old days, I thought. *Now we have angioplasty, we spar with the gods, denying inevitability.* And then, my personal mantra: *A heart attack is a missed opportunity.*

I maneuvered the angioplasty balloon across the tight narrowing, steering it over a guide wire and down the tortuous artery. Small metallic beads marked the origins and the tip of the balloon, indicating its location within the artery. The balloon was carefully centered on the blockage, its position guided by the image visualized just a few minutes earlier. Cranking the handle on the balloon inflation device filled the balloon with dye at controlled, gradually increasing pressures. The balloon kept growing, round and tubular, except for the severely narrowed waist in its midportion.

"My chest is starting to hurt, Doc."

"We have the balloon positioned on your blockage.

It's common to feel some pain when the balloon is blown up. Can you hold on for another half minute?"

Joe's heart rate started to rise. The contour of his ECG to change, responding to the lack of blood now reaching the heart muscle. The midportion of the balloon stays pinched, in a jail of fat and plaque. I increase the inflation pressure in the balloon, but the blockage doesn't want to relent.

"Pain's worse, Doc."

The balloon has been inflated for 30 seconds, long enough to gauge how readily or reluctantly the plaque will change its contour. A sharp pull on the handle of the inflation device starts to suck the dye back out of the balloon. The sausage shrinks and gradually, the balloon again becomes a narrow thread. Blood flow is restored.

The chirping cadence of the heart monitor slowed. The ECG's contour started to normalize as oxygen again began to reach the heart muscle.

"Pain going away yet?

"Yes, it's starting to get better. That was the same feeling I was getting when I walked or was under stress."

Another bead of sweat rolled down my back. A puff of dye filled the artery, showing that the blockage had not resolved. We were not home free yet.

"I must blow the balloon up again to fix this blockage, Joe. It may hurt again."

The sequence was the same. The balloon took on the

sausage-like shape as it filled again with dye. The heart rate climbed, and the ECG contour changed. Oxygen-carrying blood cannot reach the heart muscle while the balloon is filled. Chest pain starts after about fifteen seconds.

An indentation persisted in the balloon's midportion. The blockage was hard, calcified, bone-like. The gauge said we're already at 8 atmospheres of pressure: balloon burst is rated at 8 atm. In a few years, there would be tougher balloons that can handle higher pressures. But in the mid-eighties, 8 atmospheres was the recommended limit.

Sixty seconds passed.

The ECG and chest pain were predictably worse.

"The pain's back again, Doc. I think there is more this time,"

"The balloon is up again, Joe. The blockage is pretty hard, and we need to keep working on it a bit longer."

I kept my eyes glued to the monitors, shifting back and forth between the X-ray image of the balloon, watching the wasp waist and waiting for it to expand, and the ECG blipping across the dark screen.

It was approaching decision time.

Joe shifted. He was having pain, but although he was uncomfortable, he said nothing. A good soldier, this is his job now and he will do it.

At ninety seconds, Joe's heart rate had gone from 72

up to 96. The waist in the balloon started to widen. I collapsed the balloon and began to breathe more easily as the ECG normalized.

Joe's pain receded.

As the balloon was inflated one more time, the waist suddenly popped and the sausage fills and becomes a smooth tube. A puff of dye confirms the result.

I let out a sigh of relief. "Looks good Joe, I think we got it."

I recall a different case from few weeks earlier. Another patient who had an angioplasty could not be taken past this critical point. This patient's plaque was rock-hard and would not yield. It was impossible to reconfigure the artery to relieve the blockage. Even though the balloon had been inflated to higher and higher pressures, the narrow constriction remained. It was hard, firm, calcified, and ultimately unyielding. Balloon burst again was rated at 8 atmospheres, but in our attempt to open the stubborn blockage we carefully raised the balloon pressure to 8, then 9 and 10, and gradually up to 12 atm. Each time, the ECG became threatening but returned to normal when the balloon was collapsed. If the balloon burst, the artery would likely tear. The patient would be rushed emergently to the OR in a race against time. He would need bypass surgery immediately to avert a devastating heart attack. After a very long half hour of increasing concern and the patient having repeated chest pain, success for this patient meant that he had been to the edge but had not been pushed over.

That gentleman was sent for elective surgery.

Docs joked about doing angioplasty, quoting the Kenny Rodgers song "You've got to know when to hold 'em and when to fold 'em."

But today, things were better. Joe's waist-like blockage relented. After a couple more short inflations the artery looked better. The final pictures were gratifying: the prior area of blockage now looked like a near normal artery.

"We're done Joe. The artery looks fine. We got a nice result. Are you having any pain now?"

"Pain's all gone now; I feel normal."

These words were like music. I love the snap my gloves make as I pull them off at the end of a case. Music too. The gown came off and got placed in the bio disposables bin behind the door. The lead apron, my protection from daily exposure to X-rays, was half-hung, half-tossed on the apron stand: a part of the ritual.

There was lightness, and a bit of relief mixed with satisfaction.

The electric opener swung the lab doors wide open. As always, my green scrub shirt was discolored, damp with sweat.

Joe's son looked up and saw me. He turned and

spoke to his mother. Joe and his mother rose. I extended my right arm to shake the son's hand.

We were all smiling.

16

IMPACT OF INTERVENTION

The elderly gentleman stared in my direction, trying to decide if he recognized me.

I tried to decide if I recognized him – and then, as if by reflex, I said his name.

"Saul, is that you? You look great. How many years has it been since I last saw you?"

"Dr. Kleiman? Oh my gosh! It's been so long since we last met. I'm doing so much better than before my operation. My stamina really improved. Going ahead with the surgery was the right thing for me to do."

I felt as if I had found a long-lost friend. Saul's comments confirmed that his improvement continued. And yes, I remembered correctly: the surgery Saul had when I was caring for him was a mitral heart valve replacement.

How long ago was that? I wondered. *Had so many years really passed?*

We chatted for a while, then the brief reunion was over. Yet this short interaction stirred me and left me with a deep sense of satisfaction.

Saul was eighty-one years old when I last saw him. I had moved from clinical practice back to full-time research almost five years earlier. Seeing him, I felt that his life and obvious well-being reaffirmed that the recommendation to proceed with surgery had been correct.

I certainly wouldn't have anticipated that this unexpected encounter would leave me feeling so proud. But it triggered a flood of emotions. I was able to experience the reward of seeing the impact of a decision; seeing it framed against time, attesting to its durability and correctness.

What made a good clinician? Was it the ability to hear and recognize subtle meaning hidden beneath a patient's sometimes vague complaint, symptom, or question? In those moments, must the doctor understand and integrate those clues into a recognizable framework? When is the right time to intervene, and help the body repair itself?

Sometimes, after years of experience, decisions seemed straightforward, obvious. But when I taught medical students, as I was on my way to do when I happened upon Saul, it was clear that these decisions were obvious only in the context of a background of experience and learning.

The challenge was knowing the right time to intervene, or when the best therapy was to carefully hold steady and observe, to "stay the hand" and then, at the proper time, reach the judgment that the risk of surgery was low enough to warrant moving ahead. Then, it meant working closely with the surgeon in counseling the family to proceed and, when appropriate, to proceed at a hospital near the patient's home, not at a well-known but distant medical center. Care at such a center could take the patient far away from family, away from easily available support, and away from immediate follow-up care should a problem arise after the discharge home.

The surgical and interventional branches of medicine shared a particular irony: to help a patient, the physician first had to put him at risk. Sending Saul for valve surgery would change the natural history of his disease. Without surgical intervention, he would live with a small and gradually increasing chance of heart failure or death. As his disease progressed without surgery, that risk would grow, as would the risk of operation.

On any given day, Saul's incremental risk from his heart disease was small. But on the day that he had valve surgery, the danger was acute. The risk on that day was concentrated and unavoidable. It was many times greater than the small daily incremental risk he took if he deferred his operation.

When Saul was wheeled into the OR, the dangers were no longer statistical or theoretical. At that moment, the risk became binary. He would live or die on that day or in the days following the operation. A stark and inescapable reality was present. If all went well, as it most often did, Saul's symptoms would recede, he would heal, and his risk from his heart disease would progressively lessen. So the doctor who did these procedures or made these decisions took his patients to the edge and stood on the edge *with* them. If the doctors involved were skilled, and at times also lucky, they would bring the patients back from the precipice.

* * *

Larry had been hospitalized with daily crescendo anginal chest pain. He was on the brink of a heart attack when I first saw him. A crucial artery supplying the front left side of his heart was closing off, making a potentially fatal heart attack imminent. But after the few hours it took to repair his artery with an early angioplasty procedure, he was functionally "cured." He passed his treadmill test the next day and went home shortly thereafter. That was in 1982, when the angioplasty procedure was uncommon, difficult, risky, and relatively untested. Few hospitals provided the service.

In those early days, one of approximately every three or four ended with abrupt closure of the artery being treated. The patient would be rushed to emergency bypass surgery. Despite the best efforts of engineering and physician pioneers around the world, angioplasty equipment was initially cumbersome and not user-friendly.

Procedures frequently took several hours and tested the endurance of the patient and cardiologist alike. But although the angioplasty procedure was new and relatively untried, patients readily accepted this risk since a successful angioplasty could mean that open heart surgery would not be necessary. Success meant that the patient could avoid having their chest cracked, and with it, an inescapable recovery period and midline scar – the day following the angioplasty, the patient would have only a tiny telltale needle mark in the groin area to indicate that anything had been done.

After Larry's successful angioplasty, his referring physician continued to follow him, since "all was fine." I didn't see him again for almost fifteen years. But that long-delayed follow-up visit was nothing short of miraculous. He was effusive when I finally saw him.

"Doc, before you did your angioplasty thing on me, I was having chest pain every day. I was having a hard time working and thought I was going to lose my job.

Afterward, I had no more chest pain and no more heart problems. I never did have that heart attack we were both worried about."

Larry had in fact matured uneventfully from a forty-five- to a sixty-year-old. He had done hard manual work almost every day of those fifteen years. He would soon retire. His daughter had married, and he danced at her wedding. Even after fifteen years, his ECG and treadmill stress test were normal. That brief angioplasty intervention had changed his life because it had prevented his life from changing.

Even with wild optimism and imagination, it would have been impossible to foresee the impact that angioplasty and valve surgery would have on these two lives and ultimately on thousands of others with similar cardiac problems.

> *"To save one life is as if to save an entire universe."*
>
> — THE *TALMUD*

HOURGLASS ARTERY

Dr. Norm, a recently retired chemist and former VP at a major chemical company, had been my last patient the prior afternoon, his visit scheduled urgently at the request of his family doctor.

Now he was in the cardiac catheterization lab having an emergency coronary angiogram. As the X-ray dye was injected into the first of his coronary arteries, a puff of dye refluxed from the artery into the larger aorta. The dye briefly formed a white cloud, silhouetted against the gray-black lungs. Then, the cloud was quickly washed away by the pulsing blood flow. The rest of the dye flowed forward, outlining the main left artery as a round, smooth quarter inch diameter tube.

Abruptly, the white column thinned to a fine line. A half-inch farther, the vessel filled out again, creating an hourglass shape. The dye then continued uninterrupted in its serpentine course down the pulsating heart.

I reflexively looked up at the glowing monitor screen. Dr. Norm's blood pressure and ECG were stable. *A disaster in waiting,* I thought. The narrowed vessel, the left main coronary artery, was the most critical artery supplying blood to the heart. Three quarters or more of the blood to Dr. Norm's heart was now coming through a severely diseased blood vessel that narrowed to a thread. This was the result of classic hardening of the arteries: atherosclerosis, a silent, stalking, sudden killer. An hour, day, week or month later, Dr. Norm would clutch his chest in pain and collapse, or perhaps just suddenly drop, dying with no warning.

Slow down. I took a deep breath and adjusted the control handle. The X-ray tower rotated to the other side of Dr. Norm; a second picture would show the narrowing from another angle.

"How are you feeling? Any chest discomfort?"

"I feel fine. When are you going to start?"

That was the type of answer I hoped for, since with his critical anatomy, even the angiogram posed increased risk.

With the next picture the X-ray camera again hummed its familiar soft machinery music, gears meshing, film advancing. Again the dye flowed into the main left coronary artery. Again it abruptly narrowed to outline a short segment where it became a thread.

I was walking on eggshells now. Like other cardiologists experienced in performing angiograms, I had seen patients die on the cath lab table with this type of blockage, even after only one picture had been taken. Dr. Norm had a potentially lethal blockage. This crucial artery was the sole inlet for blood supplying two of the three major arteries feeding his heart. If the main left artery blocked completely, he would die with no warning. There would be no chance to get to the operating room. The heart's vital blood supply would be cut off and there would be no life-giving oxygen to nourish its cells. It would simply stall, fail, and crash.

Dr. Norm urgently needed bypass surgery. My task now was to get enough information for the surgeon to know which arteries needed bypass, but not to put the patient at extra risk by doing more than necessary. The second view looked like the first, another hourglass-like narrowing.

I paused and ran the "instant replay" video a couple times, assuring myself that the anatomy was clearly displayed. No point in pushing my luck. The initial diagnostic question was answered, but I still needed a picture of his third, right coronary artery. Then we'd be done. So I moved ahead and finished the angiogram with a single quick right coronary artery injection. One picture was sufficient to get the additional information needed to guide the surgeon in placing the remaining bypasses.

* * *

At 4:45 p.m. the day before, I was wrapping up a long afternoon in the office. I walked into the examining room with a sigh of relief. My last office visit was with a longtime patient whom I always enjoyed seeing. Then I had a mound of lab reports to review, about seven or eight calls to return, and three patients to recheck at the hospital. If I moved along, I could be done by 7:00 p.m., dinner by 9:00 p.m., and bed by 11:00 p.m.

Georgi, my wife and office nurse, knocked on the door.

"Dr. Larry called. He has a sixty-two-year-old VIP who's leaving tomorrow for the Galapagos Islands. He's had some intermittent left arm pain. Dr. Larry took an ECG and it was abnormal. He's sending him up for you to see."

There's an adage in medical practice, and probably in other fields as well, that a consultant is someone called in to share the blame.

Along with being late for dinner, I suspected I might have the privilege of being the bad guy who had to tell a man I had never met before, that he couldn't or shouldn't go on his long-awaited vacation. Or the privilege of being held responsible if he went on his dream trip and had the proverbial Big One. Georgi stuck her head into the office again.

"Dr. Norm is here. I'll put him in a room. Do you

want me to have the ECG tech stay late in case you need to do a treadmill?" I appreciated her understanding of the situation and anticipation of what was likely to be needed.

Dr. Norm, it turned out, was irritated and irritable. He had retired a very short while ago. He was going on the trip, he insisted. Whatever needed to be done, he would take care of immediately on his return. That is, he said, if anything at all needed to be done. He had a fifteen-year dream of taking his wife on a trip to the Galapagos Islands as a retirement celebration. This was to be the first of many trips now that the burden of work had been lifted.

"I hope you'll be able to go," I offered. "Let's try to sort this out. Tell me, what's been going on that Dr. Larry sent you to see me?"

Dr. Norm's history was interesting and subtle. He liked to walk. And over the last two weeks, when he walked, he occasionally noted that his left forearm ached. "It didn't really hurt," he said. "Just an ache. Mild."

I probed, exploring his history in further detail. Did it ache when he started walking or after he had walked a while? Was the discomfort more if he walked fast or slowly? Did he perspire when it hurt? How was his breathing when the arm ache came? Was his walking pace now as fast as it had always been? Did the ache come every time he walked, or just intermittently? What happened if he stopped walking? Did the ache persist or leave? What if he walked against the wind or on a cold or on a wet day? Did it ever come at rest, or at night? Or wake him from sleep? Or occur during sex? After this questioning, I excused myself to find the ECG tech.

"We need to do a treadmill," I informed her. "Thanks for staying."

I returned to Dr. Norm and completed his medical history and performed a detailed cardiovascular exam. I looked at the ECG that Dr. Larry had sent with the patient.

Each heartbeat produces an electrical wave pattern. When the heart is activated, it generates an electrical signal that looks like a spike. As it recovers from each beat, it generates a mildly sloping coved wave. Sometimes when the heart's arteries get clogged, the pattern changes, giving a clue. But these findings are not always diagnostic since similar changes are sometimes seen when the heart is normal. Dr. Norm's wave pattern was concerning. Not clear-cut, but worrisome. I needed more information.

"Dr. Norm, I'd like to do a test called a treadmill or stress test," I said. "If it's OK with you, we'll hook you up to an ECG and watch it as you walk on the treadmill machine. We'll start slowly, and gradually increase the speed and the hill. This way we can monitor the ECG to be sure everything is OK. I'm a bit concerned that this forearm pain you're having is a warning sign that your heart may not be getting enough blood and oxygen. The treadmill will help us sort it out."

"If it's OK, can I go on the trip?" Norm asked.

"Probably so. If you get to a reasonable level of exercise without any ECG changes, we can both be reassured," I answered.

The promise of a reprieve was all the motivation Norm needed. "When do we do it? Can you do it now?"

Five minutes later, he was connected to the monitor and ready to go. I explained the mechanics of the procedure to him in more detail. The treadmill belt would begin slowly. The speed and incline would gradually be increased. I would watch and record his ECG for telltale signs that his heart was short of blood. He was to tell me if the exercise reproduced his forearm pain, or if he didn't feel well in any way.

Norm might well have some significant coronary blockages, I thought, so just to be safe I decided to start with a mild, less strenuous protocol. He stood astride the treadmill belt as the machine started, and then stepped on. His first few steps were awkward, as most folks are the first time they walk on the treadmill apparatus. But within a dozen strides he had the hang of it.

"How does it feel? Can you keep this pace up a bit?"

Norm felt fine. The digital timer said he had been walking twenty seconds. The ECG trace streamed steadily across the green monitor screen. Then the waves started to flatten, and then they sagged. Thirty-five seconds had passed, and his ECG was already abnormal. His heart rate started to climb, then it raced.

"How do you feel?" I inquired.

"Fine," came the answer. And then, "You know, I'm starting to get that feeling in my left arm."

If Norm's heart had been able to speak, it would have yelled, "I'm running out of oxygen!" The wave pattern was classic for a heart deprived of blood and oxygen. With each beat, literally beat by beat, the abnormal pattern became more extreme.

I ran a full ECG to document the abnormality. At the same time, I hit the control button to slow the belt, level the machine, and then stop the belt altogether.

"Arm pain's worse," Norm said. The belt had already stopped. I suggested that he lie down. Beads of sweat began to form on his forehead. His color drained, then he was ashen. The sweating became more pronounced.

The ECG was slowing, but the deeply sagging abnormal wave pattern persisted. I took out a nitroglycerin tablet from the bottle we kept nearby and instructed Norm to let it dissolve under his tongue.

Two more minutes passed. Dr. Norm's pain persisted. I gave him a second nitroglycerin. Slowly, he began to feel better. His ECG began to creep toward baseline. In five more minutes, he finally felt OK, and his ECG abnormalities had resolved.

"I could have walked a while longer," he said. "How did I do?"

"How do you feel now?" I asked.

"I was OK except for those last few seconds," he said. "How does it look?"

"Let me review the whole record and give Dr. Larry a call," I suggested. "Then we'll talk."

Dr. Norm had a strongly abnormal treadmill. The fact that it had changed dramatically at a very low level of exercise suggested the presence of severe blockages in the arteries nourishing his heart. To have changes like these in under a minute during the first stage of this modified protocol was ominous. I was worried about him.

The answer was straightforward. He needed an angiogram to define the presence and extent of his coronary disease. It was highly unlikely that this was a false alarm. Sometimes treadmill tests gave false positive results, but rarely, if ever, at such low levels of exercise.

Etiquette dictated that I speak with Dr. Larry before sharing the findings with Dr. Norm. But it was fortunate that he had been referred and had the test. There was no safe way for him to go on any trip, let alone to a remote region of the world. The situation needed to be sorted out. The ECG changes had come too fast and too severely, and there was no reasonable way to ignore this for two or three weeks until he returned.

That approach might mean he would not return. Certainly, if he had a heart attack on a boat in the Pacific Ocean, he would be relying on luck alone. But with the timing, and his plans to leave tomorrow, even if he had blockages that could best be treated with medicine, or even angioplasty, there was no way to have an answer in time for him to stick to his plan.

I sensed somehow that I would be asked to share the bad news with Dr. Norm. I phoned Dr. Larry to tell him the results.

"Larry," I began. "It's Jay. Thanks for sending Dr. Norm to see me. Nice guy with quite a story. Good thing you got that ECG and had him checked. Your pick-up may well have saved his life. He's not going to be happy, but there's no way he can take the trip tomorrow. He'll need an angio; his treadmill was really abnormal almost as –"

"You weren't supposed to do a treadmill!" Dr. Larry interrupted. "He's in my HMO group plan, and I didn't authorize you to do a treadmill."

Stunned silence.

So you sent a man with an abnormal ECG and a story suggestive of coronary heart pain to a cardiologist at 4:30 p.m. on the afternoon before he's scheduled to leave the country for a remote location, and the cardiologist isn't supposed to follow his medical judgment because the patient's in an HMO?

Then I recovered sufficiently from my surprise to respond.

"Well, Larry," I began, "if there's a problem with my doing the treadmill, I'll just have to eat the cost. But I figured you'd want me to do it ASAP. As you know, this guy's planning to go out of the country tomorrow morning. You sent him because he has a suspicious history and a suspicious ECG. I figured we needed some objective way to get him off the hook and let him go or convince him that he's got a real problem and needs to stay and get it worked up." Then I tried playing to Dr. Larry's potential guilt, "In fact, I kept one of my techs late to get it done today."

"Well, I'll see what I can do," Dr. Larry replied less grudgingly.

"You probably saved his life," I added.

It didn't take much, once Dr. Larry calmed, to get him on board that with the reality that the angiogram was needed and doing it emergently was appropriate. But by then I had been "assigned" to tell Dr. Norm and telling him had been difficult. His reactions were predictable. At first, he was disbelieving.

"I really don't feel bad," he said. "I promise I'll get it taken care of as soon as I get back."

Ironically, like many very intelligent patients with advanced degrees, Dr. Norm felt that he had the background to interpret the data, maybe even better than I did. He was irritated, then adamant, and unconvinced. It became clear that gentle persuasion was not working. I explained the dramatic character of his ECG changes. I persisted.

Then I dug in my heels and pushed back.

His clinical situation had crossed the invisible line.

There was no way I could responsibly allow myself to be talked out of what I knew was a medical necessity. Of course I couldn't force Norm to stay and have an angiogram. But I owed him my best clinical judgment. I generally didn't like using fear to motivate or compel patients, but this case seemed clear-cut. With these treadmill findings, Norm might just die suddenly if left untreated. I ratcheted up the argument, used the buzzwords, and pressed.

Finally, I put it simply. "Dr. Norm," I said, "I need to be clear. If you go on this trip, you run the risk of dropping dead from a heart attack out there in a boat where you can't get any meaningful medical help. If that's a risk you want to take, you can make the decision. But my best advice to you is to stay and have this evaluated. That's what I told Dr. Larry, and he agrees and wants you to stay. If you want, I can try to set up the angiogram for tomorrow, and if you don't need angioplasty or surgery after the angiogram, we can get you on your way as quickly as possible."

And then, for emphasis, "All we're trying to do is make sure your family has you around to enjoy a long retirement."

Sixteen hours later, Dr. Norm was in the cath lab. And in the cath lab everyone's hunch was confirmed; in fact, our worst fears had been borne out. His arm pain had been a clear warning.

I now faced the prospect of explaining to him that

not only did he have blocked arteries, but that they were severe and life-threatening. He needed bypass surgery as soon as possible –even this afternoon if it could be arranged. There would be no second chances. He would not survive the heart attack that this blockage was on its way to causing.

I stayed with Norm for a few minutes after completing the procedure to be sure all remained stable, then went into the adjacent office and called Dr. Larry to share the findings.

"That was a great pick-up you made, Larry," I began. "You undoubtedly saved Dr. Norm's life." Then I went on to review the findings, concluding, "He should have a bypass as soon as feasible. If that main artery closes, he will die. Do you want me to talk to him and call the surgeon to arrange it, or would you prefer to make the arrangements yourself?"

It was agreed that I should talk to Dr. Norm and, if he agreed, call the cardiac surgeon, and schedule the bypass operation.

Norm argued for a bit that nothing needed to really be done, then he tried to negotiate to delay surgery until after his trip. In a flash of common sense, I wheeled his gurney around so he could see his films. The hourglass spoke volumes – one picture stopped the arguments.

One call and a handful of questions later, the HMO authorized coronary bypass surgery on an emergency basis. Norm's surgery was done that afternoon. He was discharged from the hospital six days later.

I learned one year later that he had finally gone to the Galapagos.

No postcard ever came.

BENNY'S NAP

A stooped, elderly gentleman sat across the exam room. His skin was slightly mottled and had a faint blue hue. His wife Ruth stood up in anticipation when I walked in, and we exchanged greetings. In the same breath, Ruth both apologized for disturbing me and, as if to justify her worry, repeated her story.

I looked critically at Benny. He had been my patient for almost ten years. Ruth's call and urgency had been most unusual.

It was hard to tell if he looked any different today. His white skin had its expected blue pallor. *Was that more intense*, I wondered? It was hard to decide.

I ran through the checklist of questions, probing.

Pain?

Difficulty breathing?

Chest tightness? Fullness? Pressure?

Sweating? Dizziness?

I questioned Benny for five more minutes, continuing to explore for any symptoms. There were no obvious clues; only the complaint that Benny had slept through the football game. Not just any football game, but a Chicago Bears football game!

I walked over and reached out to hold his wrist. Supporting his arm, I felt routinely for his pulse. His skin was cool and vaguely damp. My fingers fumbled, searching. Then I found it, definite, but weak and thready. Surprised, I asked my tech to check an ECG.

"What's wrong, Jay?" Ruth asked, not able to conceal her concern.

"Let's see what his ECG shows."

With a mix of curiosity and worry I watched the pen race across the ECG paper.

Benny's heart rate was about twice normal!

* * *

Three hours earlier my pager had interrupted my morning rounds.

"Benny's not right, Jay. Can you to take a look at him today?"

I had a couple caths scheduled in the lab, and two new consults had come in. I knew it was going to be a full day. It was one of my few days without office hours.

I would really have preferred to see Benny during my regularly scheduled office time the next day.

"Benny slept through the Bears game yesterday. He never does that," Ruth explained. I heard Benny holler in the background that he was OK. Ruth ignored him.

So, yes, it was unusual that he would sleep through the Bears game. Benny was a die-hard fan. But it hardly seemed like a medical emergency.

Ruth and Benny were the ultimate considerate patients. They rarely called, and never unless something was amiss. If anything, they erred on the side of reluctance to bother me. So this call was indeed unusual.

Still, sleeping through a football game was hardly a chief complaint I'd find in any medical text. Knowing this family as I did, though, putting them off seemed risky. It was hard to imagine a more cooperative and compliant patient than Benny.

"Is anything else going on, Ruth? Is he experiencing any pain, sweating or difficulty breathing?

"Well," Ruth began, "he still doesn't look right, and he's unusually tired. And Jay, in all these years, he's never slept through the game. He looks forward to it all week."

So I was in the office three hours later.

I looked at the ECG as the tracing finished printing. I stared in disbelief. The pattern was classic and the diagnosis immediately evident. Benny's heart rhythm was ventricular tachycardia. The electrical impulse that initiated each heartbeat was not the normal, usual one. Instead, an abnormal focus had literally hijacked control of his heart rhythm and was triggering heartbeats at an abnormally fast pace. This abnormal focus was firing at 160 beats per minute rather than the usual, between approximately 65 and 90 beats per minute.

I reached for the blood pressure cuff and quickly inflated it. His blood pressure was present but barely detectable. Why this frail old man had not collapsed was not clear. Most people with the rapid irregular heart rhythm he was showing would have passed out on the spot. He'd probably been in this rhythm for more than a day. Of course, he was tired. His blood pressure was low although still minimally adequate. I nervously laughed to myself. Sleeping through Sunday football was the least of Benny's concerns – most people collapsed or even died with this.

Benny needed to be admitted to the Coronary Care Unit to have his normal heart rhythm re-established ... after a quick stop in the Emergency Room. I had considered calling 911. But the ER was only a few hundred yards away and we could move him there in less time than it would take for the EMTs to arrive. Against the odds, Benny appeared to be stable. It would be quickest for me to ease him into a wheelchair and walk the short distance with him. Medico-legally, this wasn't by the book, but the small risk would be no different whether he waited for the EMTs in the office or was moved to the ER in similar time.

I elected to stay with Benny, and paged the resident from the CCU.

"Meet me in the ER," I instructed. "I'm bringing over a patient in ventricular tachycardia. He's clipping along at 160 beats per minute but is alert and is holding his blood pressure. We'll get him admitted and then bring him up to the Coronary Care Unit."

I turned back to Ruth. "You know your Benny well, Ruth. Come on with me, we're taking a little trip. I'll explain as we walk." At the end of the hall outside my office there was a wheelchair. I quickly wheeled Benny down the hall, into the elevator, and across the driveway that separated the office from the ER entrance. I suppose we were a bit of a sight coming in, me with my gray lab coat flying as I navigated the wheelchair at full gait through the electric doors, Benny clutching the chair's arms, and Ruth hurrying to keep up with me.

Less than thirty minutes after I saw his ECG in the exam room, Benny was in bed in the CCU with the cardiac monitor connected. He had oxygen running into his nose via a cannula. He was still maintaining his blood pressure despite his abnormal rhythm, so I decided to try using medications to convert him back to a normal heartbeat.

One after another, I tried several likely drug infusions. I filled the syringe with medication, pushed the liquid through his IV, and waited, eyes glued to the monitor. Thirty, then sixty, seconds would pass, but his ECG remained abnormal, gyrating wildly at its rapid pace. Two minutes passed without a remission. I tried a second dose. Push, watch, wait. Then I tried a third dose and waited some more. Meanwhile, we kept checking Benny's blood pressure and talking to him.

After half an hour and a full trial of two different IV medications, nothing had changed. Benny's heart was still clipping along at 160, and his BP was faint. All the while, he continued to protest that he felt fine. "Can I go home yet?" was his refrain.

I walked out of the CCU to the waiting area where Ruth sat, impatient. Anxiety showing, she again rose to greet me, questioning.

"He's not responding to the IV medications," I began. "He's still feeling OK, and so I first wanted to try to fix his rapid heart rhythm using IV medications, but he's not responding. We can't leave him like this. It's not a rhythm that will stay stable indefinitely. We're going to do a procedure called cardioversion. We'll put Benny to sleep for five minutes and use a brief electric shock to convert his heartbeat back to its normal rhythm."

The questions were always the same. How much risk? And what was the chance for success?

Back in the CCU, the anesthesiologist stood by patiently as the procedure was explained to Benny.

Some patients pepper you with questions. To others,

it's simple. They have decided that you are their advocate. They have reached trust. Benny was in the latter group; he had made his decision long ago. The conversation was very short.

"Do what you need, Doc," was the extent of his discussion. The anesthesiologist injected small amounts of a barbiturate to induce brief sleep, and I watched as Benny's eyes grew heavy and his lids sagged.

The procedure to convert his heart rhythm with an electric shock was well established and routine. I spread electrical conducting gel liberally on the paddles and pressed one paddle on the front of his chest and the second one on the side along the rib cage. A quick test synchronized the defibrillator machine with Benny's rhythm pattern.

My eyes were fixed to the monitor now. It was routine but there was always the possibility that something would go awry. In unison, my thumbs depressed the buttons on the top of each paddle. There was a split-second delay, and then a soft pop. Benny lurched upward a few inches as the electric discharge caused his muscles to contract involuntarily. Seven or eight pairs of eyes now stared expectantly at the monitor.

It was always like this.

Flat line.

A second, and then another second, dragged on. The light beam tracing Benny's ECG continued as a flat line where moments earlier it had shown wild, chaotic activity. As if exhausted by prior excess, his heart was passive now, perhaps waiting to be told what to do. I thought of Ruth sitting expectantly outside. *This scares me every time it happens. It takes faith to watch that flat line and wait.*

Three seconds passed. Then there was a blip. A single heartbeat. And another pause. And then another beat, and finally another. In another fifteen seconds, Benny's ECG was normal again. Sixty-five beats a minute. His blood pressure climbed toward 130, also normal. He moaned and tried to sit up.

I walked out of the unit and sat down in the chair beside Ruth.

"He's fine," I said smiling. "He's back in his normal heart rhythm again. And you're a smart Doc," I said. "And Ruthie," I added quickly as I rose, "Thank you for calling."

WHEN IN DOUBT

Bob's back had been hurting for a few weeks. It started as a mild occasional ache, but recently it had become more frequent and insistent. A friend at work noticed him grimacing. "Maybe it's your stomach. Try these," he offered, and tossed Bob a roll of antacids.

At first Bob thought they might have helped. He wasn't quite sure what to do next. He didn't have a personal physician. His son Norman had completed three years of medical school, and Bob thought about calling him. But he hadn't gotten around to it. Norman was always busy, immersed in studies. Bob hated to be a bother. He figured he would call if it got worse.

Tonight the pain seemed to be increasing. Norman wasn't home, and when Bob went looking for more of the chalky pills, he could find none. He tried to go to sleep at around 10:00 p.m. but couldn't seem to find a comfortable position. By 1 a.m., he was really starting to feel bad. He decided to see if he could find something to take at the all-night convenience store.

Bob had driven two blocks and was crossing the first large intersection when a swelling filled his chest. Then his chest was full, expanding, cutting off his air. The back pain returned, and quickly became excruciating. His vision blurred. He collapsed and slumped over the steering wheel as things went black.

* * *

A few miles away, Steve and his police partner were finally enjoying a quiet night. The radio messages were infrequent, and none had been directed at them. He was relishing the quiet. Winter was almost past, and with it the threat of snow and endless accidents that clogged even those nights not filled by big-city mayhem. He was moderately irritated when the call came asking him to investigate a motor vehicle accident just down the road.

A car jutted obliquely into the road, its front end crumpled. Glass shards were scattered over the pavement. A few people walked aimlessly nearby. Steve turned on his roof flasher and pulled over to look more closely.

A middle-aged man was slumped over the steering wheel. He was wearing a seat belt. His head did not show signs of having hit the windshield or wheel. In fact, he did not appear to have suffered any trauma at all. Steve reached in and shook him lightly, and then yelled a few words at him. The man groaned but did not answer coherently.

Probably damn drunk, Steve thought as he looked more closely at the scene. He reached in and found the man's pulse, feeling reassured by this as he noted another squad car pull alongside.

"Hey, do me a favor," he said to the driver, whom he thought he recognized. "Guy's a drunk or fell asleep at the wheel. Help me throw him in your back seat and run him down to the ER. He doesn't look hurt bad. I don't want to wait for an ambulance and deal with that mess."

They half-dragged, half-carried the man from his car. The man was making minimal efforts to walk, moaning a bit as they proceeded. The two policemen eased him across the back seat of the second squad car. Then, with sirens wailing and flashers pulsing, the car disappeared down the deserted boulevard.

The ER charge nurse heard the siren in the distance. She was hardly surprised when the eerie flashing lights ricocheted off the automatic glass doors. She yelled down the hall to alert the doctor on duty, took a deep breath, and waited.

* * *

It had started as a quiet enough night. Then there was a phone call that was straightforward to take care of and I fell back to sleep, confident that my decision was correct.

The second call changed everything.

Now I was rushing to get to the hospital, throwing on my clothes and then driving as fast as I dared, not wanting the cops to stop me and create an unnecessary delay.

It was easy to tell where to go because everyone was milling around. I walked hurriedly toward the throng, feeling the familiar rush, my focus growing in intensity, narrowing the world until it seemed I saw nothing but the figure lying there. The man, Bob, was ashen and mottled. Sweat poured from him in beads that ran quickly off his blue-latticed skin.

Now there was the realization of sudden responsibility. My mind was racing, considering possibilities, trying to connect the clinical pieces into a coherent picture.

The situation was not as it had been described to me an hour earlier. The man looked as if he was dying. The ER had put him in mast pants, like the astronauts wear in the face of high G forces, to maintain his blood pressure. They made his legs look bubble wrapped. The rhythmic inflation and deflation of the air pockets seemed almost comical amid the growing activity. I checked and found he barely had a blood pressure. It was difficult to detect despite two IVs pouring fluid into him through large bore needles.

The ER nurse began to explain. "The cops brought him in after a minor accident. Fender-bender type."

"Any trauma?"

"No, he barely collided, but he lost consciousness. His ECG showed a small heart attack on the bottom side of his heart." The small heart attack seemed to have caused a clinical crisis. Or was there some other problem?

"Lab, blood counts, OK?"

"They seem to be," the nurse replied.

The ER doctor had called me for the first time a little more than an hour earlier. As part of the initial emergency management of Bob's heart attack, he wanted to give Bob a clot-busting drug to open the clogged artery that was the cause of his heart attack.

This drug, abbreviated TPA, was relatively new. It had generated considerable excitement in the medical community. When given in the early hours following the onset of a heart attack, it could dissolve the culprit clot that had blocked an atherosclerotic blood vessel. This reestablished blood flow to the jeopardized heart muscle and usually aborted, or at least limited, the size of the heart attack. The healing power of TPA came with a price, however. The "clot-busting" power of the drug was generalized and indiscriminate: it could induce unwanted dangerous bleeding at sites other than the target vessel. This was particularly dangerous if the recipient had suffered injury or trauma.

The ER doc had enthusiastically advocated that TPA be given.

Although Bob had no visible evidence of traumatic injury due to his auto crash, it was possible he had sustained internal injuries that were not immediately apparent. These could bleed dangerously under the influence of clot-busting TPA.

During that first conversation the ER doc had really pushed the idea. "Bob is a pretty young guy," he said. "He has no ECG evidence of prior heart problems. He's a good candidate for TPA. It may help him stay strong as he ages."

"Yes," I said, "but we can't be certain that his auto accident hasn't caused some internal injury that we can't see. If so, administering TPA would put him at risk for major bleeding. Most people survive the kind of heart attach he has without difficulty. You've told me he's been stable since arriving here. It's not worth the risk."

I wanted to look at his ECG again. The changes indicating his heart attack were localized and suggested that only a small amount of heart muscle was injured. People with heart attacks on the bottom of their hearts usually do well. "If Bob hadn't been in a car crash, I would agree to TPA. But not in this case," I said firmly.

In fact, I had considered the possibility of administering TPA once again as I was driving to the hospital. But rethinking the decision had made me more resolute. TPA paralyzed the blood clotting system. A patient could bleed uncontrollably if his blood was "thinned" and there had been even some minor unnoticed injury. The risk of bleeding outweighed the risk of his relatively small heart attack.

After this conversation in the ER, I began to examine Bob. Unexpectedly, his belly was stiff and rigid with involuntary muscle spasm. It felt hard and tense, as though he was pushing back against my probing fingers with all his strength. This was reflex; he wasn't consciously doing so. These findings suggested a critical abdominal process independent of his heart attack.

By chance, the surgeon on ER call had been called in to see another patient. This was fortunate because delay could further endanger Bob.

"Art, can you take a look at this patient?" I asked the surgeon. "It looks like he's got an acute abdomen. But it doesn't make sense that his blood pressure is crashing like this unless he's bleeding or has some internal disaster."

Just then, the ER nurse told me that Bob's two adult children were in the waiting room. No one had talked to them. While Art assessed Bob, I went to find them.

Bob was divorced, and these young adults were his only family. The older son was in medical school and planned on doing surgery training when he graduated. I updated both children on their dad's condition. As I was finishing this conversation, Art called me back into the ER. There had been blood return when he probed Bob's abdominal cavity with a long needle. This implied that our patient was bleeding internally. Based on his fragile condition and associated low blood pressure, he was probably bleeding quite heavily.

The police had told the ER doc that the patient had barely dented his fender. This made it unlikely that Bob was bleeding from a new traumatic injury. Although he could have ruptured his spleen, this was unlikely with minor trauma. *Could he perhaps have ruptured his aorta even before his accident?* In any case, one thing was clear. Heart attack or not, he needed to get to the OR as soon as we could assemble the OR team. Even though it was now 3:00 a.m., we couldn't wait for the morning shift to come in

I found the children again and further updated them on our findings and thoughts. By now, we were near certain that he was bleeding internally; we were not sure from what site. It was also now clear that the decision not to administer TPA had been crucial and correct. Given that he had dropped his blood pressure and was hemorrhaging, he almost certainly would have bled to death.

Surgical exploration of Bob's abdomen was now

urgent. Perhaps he had ruptured his aorta. If so, this would be catastrophic!

As I thought silently about the unfolding situation, I reflected that Bob was in grave danger. I hoped he would survive. I also dreaded having to tell his children that their father had not made it.

Things were speeding up now that the decision had been made to explore Bob's abdomen. The ER team knew we needed to move quickly for him to have a chance. In a few minutes we were walking and jogging the gurney down the halls to the elevator that would bring us to the OR. A nurse stood there like a sentinel, holding the elevator door open. While we were transporting the patient, the OR was setting up and I went to call the vascular surgeon. Art was a general surgeon, and if the bleeding source was a ruptured aorta, we would need a surgeon with vascular expertise.

To my chagrin, the vascular surgeon was both sleepy and irritated, snapping, "You don't really know what the hell's going on. I'm not coming in until you know, so call me back if you need me!" and hanging up. Realizing that it made more sense for me to help Art than argue, I went back to the OR. This would take only a few minutes. Bob just had to hold on a bit longer while Art surgically explored his abdomen.

A possible clinical sequence was starting to come together in my mind. Bob could have passed out when his aorta ruptured. The heart attack most likely came at nearly the same time, possibly precipitated by the initial fall in his blood pressure. The bleeding probably intensified between the first routine call and the desperate second call.

I hurried back to the OR to scrub in and help Art. Time was critical. Even though I was not a surgeon, it was 3:00 a.m. and I was available. I had enough surgical experience to assist. It was also helpful to be present to monitor Bob's heart, since there would be increased risk for surgery done in the period immediately surrounding his heart attack.

Art was quick and purposeful. He soon established visualization deep into Bob's belly. A dark blue purple area became apparent where leaking blood had carved a channel inward, next to and along the back muscles.

Bob's aorta had in fact ruptured. Fortunately, this rupture had taken the form of a slow tear rather than an explosive burst. Because the initial blood leak had worked its way along the tough lining between the back and the abdominal cavity, at first it was contained and gradual. This was critical. If the initial rupture had been directed forward into the main abdominal cavity, Bob would have bled to death in minutes. The more gradual bleed bought him a few hours, which proved to be lifesaving.

After exploring the abdominal cavity for several minutes, Art found a tear in the aorta. He struggled initially but was gradually able to slow the bleeding. In a few more minutes he was able to gain control of the situation. I left the sterile OR and went to call the vascular surgeon again. He must have felt some pangs of conscience because he came awake right away and didn't argue this time. I told him our findings; his sole response was a terse, "I'll be right in!"

Once Art had stopped the bleeding, we were able to slow the IV fluids. With the infusion of these fluids, Bob's blood pressure stabilized. A short while later, the vascular surgeon arrived and came into the OR without too much flourish. Because Art, the general surgeon, had controlled the bleeding, the vascular surgeon was quickly able to visualize the anatomy and began to repair the tear immediately. This involved sewing a long Gore-Tex tube graft that would bypass the leak in the aorta. The tube graft provided a direct channel for the blood to flow to the abdominal organs and his legs.

Two hours later the surgery was complete, and I shared the good news with Bob's children.

Bob ended up spending seven days in Intensive Care and then a week more in the hospital before he went home. But most importantly: he was discharged home. He walked out of the hospital under his own power. He had no residual deficits; his brain and kidneys were functioning normally. His survival and recovery had been miraculous.

In general, the mortality from aortic rupture outside of a hospital is well over 90 percent. But several fortunate factors had come together and had led to Bob's survival.

The time from Bob's aortic rupture until he reached a capable hospital had been less than an hour. It was recognized that neither his heart attack nor auto accident had been life-threatening. Art, the on-call surgeon was already in the hospital.

The determination that Bob's heart attack was not responsible for his subsequent sudden deterioration was critical. The conclusion that he had sustained an abdominal catastrophe was based on my bedside physical examination and led to immediate surgical exploration. Once the diagnosis of a ruptured aortic aneurysm was certain, a vascular surgeon had come to the hospital with minimal delay.

Finally, the decision *not* to administer clot busting TPA prevented uncontrollable hemorrhage.

I saw Bob on a routine basis in the office for a number of years. Approximately ten years after his surgery I received a New Year's card with a letter from him. His son had finished medical school and had completed training as a vascular surgeon. His daughter had married, and he now was the proud grandfather of two.

In the letter, Bob said that in spite of his semiconscious state, he remembered overhearing a conversation between me and the ER physician. In this conversation, the ER physician had been trying to convince me to administer TPA because of the heart attack. He quoted me as refusing and saying, "I don't want to take a chance of killing this man."

Bob also said, "my son told me that if I was taken to another hospital, I would be dead now. The difference was Dr. Kleiman at St. Joseph Hospital, and he refused to thin my blood." He concluded his note by writing, "The day does not pass that I turn my head skyward and thank God for his gifts of mercy and a few words for you. Before closing, the first thing my son, now a vascular surgeon, checks a patient for is physical signs of swelling on all main arteries looking for signs of aneurysm. My sincere thanks and admiration."

Thirty or more years after my emergency treatment of Bob, the writing of this book stirred me to attempt to reach his son, Norman. I was retired, and from time to time looked back on my years in practice both from the perspective of a figurative thirty thousand feet and with a degree of curiosity about the impact of my interaction with some of my more unusual and challenging patients. With the help of Google and recalling that Bob had told me that his son aspired to be a vascular surgeon, I was easily able to identify and then write to Norman.

I learned from him that Bob had lived another twenty years after the surgery. He had seen Norman complete medical school and his advanced medical training. Norman was in fact now a vascular surgeon at a major university medical center and remembered well the night that his father ruptured his aorta and had emergency surgery.

Communicating directly with Norman, and verifying that he had completed his specialized medical education as a vascular surgeon, was most gratifying. This contact completed the circle for me and showed me that I had helped to pass the baton to the next generation.

20

TIMING IS ALL

Dr. Max had immigrated to the United States as a young man shortly after he completed his medical and surgical training. He was an "old-school" doctor, with broad skills in general medicine and primary care, as well as specialized competence in general surgery. His manner was gracious. He was committed to personally caring for his patients and sought to address their emotional as well as medical needs. From time to time, he would ask me to see a patient in cardiac consultation. It was not unusual that he asked me to consult on a patient of his who had a heart murmur that required evaluation.

"Jay," Dr. Max began. "There's an interesting patient I'd like you to see. He's had a heart murmur since I first saw him three years ago. It's more prominent now than it initially was, and I'm not sure if we should just continue to observe him, or if it's time for him to have additional testing or an intervention."

Herb was fifty-eight years old and denied any pain or shortness of breath either at rest or with exertion. I asked whether he was working or retired. This information might give me insight into his physical condition, particularly if he was still working on a job that required stamina or exertion.

"He retired a couple of years ago. He had been on the same administrative job for thirty years and was able to retire on a full pension. I don't think fatigue or exertional limitation impacted his decision," Dr. Max replied. "He's going home today after a minor surgical procedure. Can you meet him before he leaves and set up an outpatient office visit?"

I went to Herb's hospital room as he was getting ready for discharge. He was still having some postoperative pain but had already dressed in anticipation of going home.

"Good morning," I began. "I'm Dr. Kleiman, a heart specialist. Dr. Max asked me to see you in my office once you've recovered from your surgery." As I introduced myself, it became clear that Herb would need to rest several weeks before seeing me.

"You have some extra sounds coming from your heart that we need to evaluate. I'll schedule you for an office visit to see me in three to four weeks. Dr. Max tells me that you are not having any shortness of breath, chest pain or leg swelling. If any of these symptoms occur, call me, and I will be happy to see you sooner. My associate and I are available 24/7 for emergencies. Otherwise, I'll see you in the office after you've recovered fully from your surgery. I don't expect any surprises." Then, for emphasis, I repeated, "Call if something comes up unexpectedly and you need to be seen more urgently."

My curiosity about his condition had been piqued. I quickly asked him, "have you had any heart tests while you were hospitalized or before having surgery?"

"Just one," Herb answered. "It was a sound wave picture of my heart and its blood flow. An echocardiogram, I believe."

"Very good. I'll take a look at it," I said.

I contacted my office and scheduled Herb's initial office visit. I handed him a business card with the appointment date and time and the office 24-hour emergency telephone numbers.

The echocardiogram was a test that generated a picture of the heart and its valves by bouncing sound waves off the heart's structures, much like radar. A computer integrated the reflected waves and transformed them into images. All four chambers of the heart were typically visualized, as were the four valves that normally kept blood flowing in a forward direction. Leaking heart valves and weakened or enlarged heart pumping chambers typically could be visualized.

I called the echo lab and had them set Herb's echocardiogram aside for me to review. It proved to be very informative. It demonstrated a mild to moderate "leak" across the mitral valve, the valve that lies between the left atrium and the left ventricle. These two chambers work together. The left atrium collects blood which has been oxygenated in the lungs. The left ventricle pumps this oxygenated blood to all body organs and tissues.

A month passed, and Herb came for his scheduled visit. He was about six feet tall, thin, with greying hair. Herb had been a middle-level manager in a manufacturing company, with administrative responsibilities that did not require physical exertion.

"Do you feel like you've completely recovered from your surgery?" I asked.

"I think so," Herb answered.

"Are you doing all the activities that you did before?"

"Again, I think so."

"What's the most physically active thing you do?" I asked.

Herb had a hobby that was totally new to me.

"I look for lost objects made of metal or containing metal, things that are often interesting and occasionally valuable," he said.

Herb was what people sometimes call a detectorist. "It involves a great deal of walking," he told me. "I go to an area where interesting objects may have been dropped or unintentionally buried, like a sports field, for example. I walk carefully over places like that with a metal detector. The detector is fairly heavy now that you mention it. It takes effort to guide it over the ground, particularly on uneven or sloping areas. If the detector signals that something metal is buried, I stop and dig it out. That's where the hobby's name comes from."

"Do you walk slowly?"

"You have to," Herb said. "Otherwise, you miss things. Overall, I think my energy is back like it was before surgery. Did you see my earlier echocardiogram? How did it look?"

I had seen a definite leak in one of his heart valves. The leak was causing the extra sounds, a heart murmur that I could hear with my stethoscope. "These sounds come from the turbulence caused by the leak. It's somewhat like the whitewater you see around a waterfall."

"How bad does it look?" Herb asked.

"It's moderate," I replied. "Your heart's main left heart pumping chamber is slightly enlarged. This is because of the extra work it does to pump blood that flows backward instead of forward. Your heart can compensate now, but most likely you'll eventually need heart surgery to have an artificial valve placed. These days, it's a common and successful operation. You would typically be in the hospital about a week. Most people are back to full function in three months."

Herb wanted to know how I could tell when someone needed surgery.

"The decision is based on several things. I'll see you in the office every two to three months. We look for changes in your breathing and stamina. The heart murmur often gets longer and louder. We also follow your echocardiogram to look for changes in the severity of your valve leak and in the size of your heart's pumping chambers. Patients often have a long stable period but then develop symptoms more rapidly. Based on your activity level and echo results, it will probably be a year or more before we have to make that decision. Of course, if symptoms develop or get worse between visits, you need to call us right away!

"Now, let's take a listen and examine you." I took my stethoscope out of my grey coat pocket, warmed up the head and positioned Herb for a full exam. His physical findings and echo suggested early to mid-severity of his mitral valve leak. I shared the information with him, telling him that I wanted to see him every two months in the office so we could follow his clinical course.

* * *

For the first year, I saw Herb every two months. As he proved to be stable, the interval between his visits stretched to three months. He had echocardiograms annually. After several years, a small, but definite increase in the chamber size appeared. The frequency of his visits was increased back to every two months.

One winter night, when the temperatures hovered in the high teens, Herb paged me sometime after midnight. "Doc," he began, "for the past couple of days since we've had this cold spell, I've noticed that I'm becoming winded when I walked much shorter distances than usual. And it's happening even if I slow my pace way down. I've been stopping to rest even if I walk only a half block or so."

"Do you catch your breath right away?" I asked. "Do you have any chest pain when you get these episodes?"

"No, it's just been my breathing," Herb answered. "Tonight, I was out for a walk, not doing anything in particular. It was just a cold night, and I was enjoying breathing the crisp, cold air. Suddenly, my breath got really short. I had to wait a long time to be able to go on and get home. Once I got home, I tried to lie down but that made me winded, and I had to sit up to be comfortable."

"How is your breathing now?"

"It's pretty much back to normal. I'm taking it very easy and I'm OK as long as I move slowly. I waited a couple hours before calling you and have had only a bit of restless sleep on and off."

I looked at my watch. It was 2:00 a.m.

"Herb, I think your heart and leaky valve may have reached a tipping point. Your heart may no longer be able to compensate for the extra work the leaky valve is causing. We need to get you to the hospital where you'll be safe. Then we'll reevaluate your condition. I'll call the ER and tell them you're on your way." I didn't believe it would be safe for him to drive himself and asked him to have a friend drive. "If you develop any more shortness of breath or chest pain, or your friend is not available, call an ambulance right away."

By now I was fully awake and trying to think through what might have led to his changed condition. Given the time that had passed since I first met him, it was possible that we were seeing the natural progression of his underlying disease. Perhaps his heart was tiring from pumping the extra blood volume. The added stress of tonight's cold conditions may have pushed him over the edge. *Time to reevaluate.*

I caught up with Herb in the ER, where the nurses were getting ready to transfer him to the CCU. Although he appeared relatively comfortable, his breathing was still slightly rapid, as was his pulse rate. The head of his bed was raised to a sitting position. I wanted to speak with him to see if I could identify any event that might have precipitated this change in status.

"Herb, has anything changed in your daily routine since I last saw you? Have you been sick, running a fever or feeling unwell in the past week or two?" I asked.

"No, Doc," he answered. "Maybe I've been getting

tired more easily when I walk with my metal detector. But it's been gradual."

"What about your diet? Have you taken in a lot of salty foods in the past few days or so?"

"Nope."

"Let me listen to your heart and lungs before you're transferred. Then I'll see you once you're settled into the CCU," I said.

Herb sat up and leaned forward so I could listen to his lungs. As I had suspected, there were telltale fine crackles over both sides of his lower back. These "rales" were caused by slight fluid accumulation in the air sacs inside his lungs. Herb's heart murmur was now more prominent and of longer duration. It had definitely changed since his last office visit. I sat down at the central desk and ordered routine laboratory tests, chest X-ray and ECG, and an echo. I scheduled time for me to do a heart catheterization in the morning and spoke to Dr. Max, Herb's referring physician, to give him an update. These test results would determine the need for mitral valve replacement surgery.

Late that afternoon, results in hand, I went to Herb's room. It was time to sit down with him and discuss the findings together. Often this would be a time when family members such as spouses or adult children were present, but Herb was single, and so the discussion was between just the two of us.

"Herb, it looks like we have some answers and also

need to make some decisions," I began. "Your valve leak has gotten worse since we first met. It is now severely stressing your heart. If we don't fix it, it will continue to enlarge and weaken your heart's pumping chamber. As you know, we've followed your condition for several years, and during that time things remained stable, with no significant change. Based on the tests we've just run, it's time to replace the leaking valve before it does significant permanent damage. The good news is that the heart catheterization showed that the arteries supplying your heart with blood are normal. You won't need a coronary artery bypass when they replace your valve— 'only' valve replacement."

Herb interrupted even before I could finish. In his understandable concern he formed questions almost faster than he could speak them. "That sounds like a big operation. How dangerous is it? Would you do it here? How long would it take for me to recover?"

I tried to slow things down.

"Herb, those are good questions. Let me answer them one at a time. The success rate for this operation for someone like you is better than 95 percent. In part that is because you would be having your operation while you are relatively young and strong, and the leak is only now beginning to significantly weaken your heart. We have a very good heart surgery team at this hospital, and I'd like them to see you. You can expect to be in the hospital for about five to seven days. While you will get stronger and feel better day by day, I tell people that by about three months you will be back to full activity, although your stamina will start to improve immediately. Dr. Max agrees with the decision for surgery. I'm sure you'll think of more questions, so write them down and I'll come by this evening. You will have another chance to get them answered."

Herb's earlier episode of "air hunger" on the cold winter night was sufficiently dramatic that he accepted the need for an intervention. He had, in fact had a mild, reversible episode of heart failure. He was ready, and even anxious, to go forward. His operation was scheduled for the next morning. His operative course went very well. Recovery went smoothly and there were no complications. He was discharged home in one week.

Six weeks later, Herb cautiously resumed his "detectorist" activities. Over the ensuing three months his stamina progressively normalized. He continued to be followed as an outpatient, and his heart condition remained stable, as documented clinically, and with annual echocardiograms. He required no further cardiac interventions.

* * *

Why did I tell this story? Herb's clinical course was typical of my patients with valvular heart disease. There was an initial period of "getting to know the patient."

The first step was exploration of their clinical and social history and physical findings. Next was a thorough review of past medical records and lab and imaging. Herb and I developed a working partnership in which he was educated to the natural history of his disease. This process facilitated the flow of clinical information between us, and Herb helped monitor his own clinical status. It was critical that he feel comfortable reaching out to me with questions or observations. I found these often contained clinically valuable, or even critical information.

A key part of this process was removing firewalls that limited direct contact between doctor and patient. In over thirty years of clinical practice, I found that facilitating a patient's ability to communicate with me, as their caregiver, was access rarely abused. Ease of communication often made it easier for me to deliver high-quality, personalized care. Herb's case illustrates this. He had regular and routine physician access, but also appropriately reached out for help and readily received it when his status changed. He had been educated sufficiently in the anticipated course of his disease so that he was able to recognize a critical change and convey this to me. The bond we developed over time proved to be life-changing.

Has this important dialogue been lost in today's corporatization of medicine? Hopefully not, but we should strive to maintain ease of access and communication as essential elements of quality care. We should also educate our patients on their disease process so that they become a helpful partner. This working relationship based on trust and the bond formed with patients helps in the delivery of optimal medical services. Herb and I had this bond. He knew when there was a change and called at the appropriate time. Patient education served us both well.

21

HEARING THE MUSIC

The surgeon was waiting for me when I doubled back to the Emergency Room.

"He's got a roaring gallbladder infection and needs IV antibiotics to cool it down. Then his gallbladder is coming out. He's very sick. Much longer, and the infection would have probably broken through into his bloodstream," he said.

"Did you tell him yet?" I asked.

"No, I was waiting to talk to you. We can tell him together."

A few hours earlier I had called Dave for the second time that morning. By the end of that call, I had given him a simple directive: "Grab a cab or get someone to drive you to the Emergency Room. I need to see you right away."

"OK," he said. No questions, no discussion. Just a soft

"OK." Dave's response removed my lingering concern that I was overreacting.

Dave was a tough – but gentle – longtime friend. When he was younger, he'd served in the Marine Corps. Over time he had become like an uncle or brother who was part of the fabric of my life. He was the kind of guy I could imagine bounding out of the woods in the dead of night after some weeklong clandestine operation, still smiling, revved, and ready to go. You'd probably describe Dave as ready for just about any assignment. A big guy, burly at about six feet and 250 pounds, he was built to last. If you were casting for a remake of the *Dirty Dozen* or had some tough physical challenge, you'd pick Dave to be part of your team.

I met Dave when my children were having a hard time, struggling with adolescence and the fallout from my divorce. He had been referred to me as a counselor for my kids. It was soon evident that, though tough and sometimes gruff, Dave had a heart of gold. He sincerely cared. He empathized with others' pain and acknowledged it. Things *mattered* to him.

Gradually we became friends, and eventually, very good friends. Sometimes Dave would challenge me. Being a physician, I lived in a world of science and data, of cause and effect – a world where actions and outcomes were supposed to be predictable. It was an article of faith that events followed rules that could be described and understood. Real things could be documented, made tangible, or at least tagged with some marker so they could be seen, counted, or traced. That was part of the beauty I saw in science.

Dave was a psychologist. His world focused on the intangible, the less quantitative and well-measured; it was a world of feeling and nuance. Words were sometimes shadows, a code perhaps unknown even to the speaker. It was to be expected that things were not always as stated, there could be hidden dimensions, distortions, or deceptions, whether intended or unintended. And in the same way Dave sometimes laughed at my literal interpretations, I marveled at his intuitiveness.

I used to call Dave from time to time when I'd be driving to the hospital in the early morning. Slow, crawling traffic became an opportunity to visit. It was a good time to catch him when we both could talk, since he generally saw clients at night, and I'd usually get home at the time he was busiest in his office.

So it really was random and not the least bit unusual that I dialed Dave one morning on my way to the hospital. What was strange though, was that Dave sounded far away. That struck me. His voice was softer than usual. It wasn't just the car phone connection, but his spark seemed gone. It was almost as if the volume control on his life's energy had been turned down.

When I commented, Dave replied that he thought he had "a touch of the flu." He had no appetite, a little fever, a little nausea. He was waiting for a callback from his doctor.

We chatted. I didn't focus too much on Dave's flu. It didn't seem extraordinary. The conversation helped pass the time on an otherwise slow and tedious creep toward the hospital. On this morning the traffic was so snarled that I rarely shifted out of first and into second gear.

When I finally reached the hospital my day began with the usual rounds, the expected patient visits, hallway discussions, pages, and telephone calls.

But somehow, the call to Dave started replaying in my mind. Subliminally, at first, like soft elevator music. But it persisted, then grew dissonant and unsettling. I became aware again that Dave had been strangely subdued. There was no bounce in his voice; no energy, inflection, or volume. He was uncharacteristically flat. Big old bulldog Dave sounded *so* tired, *so* laid back, *so* soft-spoken, *so passive*. I reached for a cup of coffee and sat down at the nursing station to dial again.

"So, how long have you been sick?" I asked.

"About a week or two. I had some tests a couple days ago. I was waiting to hear back from my doctor about them."

"You've been feeling bad that long? What kind of tests did you have?"

"Well, I've been having some nausea off and on, and not much of an appetite for the past couple weeks. The test I took was terrible, very painful. Some sort of ultrasound."

I realized that the test Dave was describing was an ultrasound of his gallbladder. Ultrasounds are not painful. The test would have involved touching his belly with a transducer the size of a small plum and coated with gel lubricant. The procedure generated a picture using sound waves. It really should not have hurt at all.

This conversation was not reassuring. I began to consider that my good friend might be harboring something more than the flu.

"So, tell me more about this ultrasound test you had." I inquired.

"Oh, they ran a small probe along my belly, under the ribs. It was the most painful thing I can remember in a long time." Dave answered softly.

"Right or left side?"

"Right."

Bingo. The pieces fit together and made sense.

"Dave, I need to see you at the hospital."

It wasn't surprising to me a bit later when the surgeon confirmed my impression. What was surprising was how abnormal Dave's blood profile was, in contrast to his minimal symptoms. His temperature was now over 102. His white blood count was three times normal.

Dave had a severe gallbladder infection.

We talked about it a few weeks after his successful

surgery. The affirmation from Dave came when he asked, "How did you know? I didn't give you any data," he joked. "How did you figure I was so sick?"

"The weakness of your voice was data to me. You not having your usual spark was data to me. The pain with the ultrasound when there should have been none, was dramatic data to me. It became obvious when you gave me all the pieces," I said.

"So now you can understand what I do," Dave said with a chuckle. "I listen for the music beneath the words. It was important that you heard more than the words. I was much sicker than either of us first realized."

We didn't talk too much about the episode after that. I just remained grateful that it had turned out well, that through some quirk of fate I had happened to call Dave that day, and that it was possible to decipher the hidden message. What he had been experiencing turned out to be far more than the usual flu.

As I continued my practice, from time to time, other clinical cases presented in ways that were not direct or obvious. These might involve illnesses where the predominant feature was unusual or understated. In Dave's case, the ability to bore down on subtle, obscure clues redirected my attention to an otherwise hidden diagnosis.

Thinking of the introduction to physical diagnosis and clinical history taking first articulated in the Blue Book, I remembered the listing of symptoms that initially seemed so vague to me as to be meaningless. With experience, it became clear that on occasion the physician needed to focus on subtleties. This realization emphasized the import of interactions between doctor and patient. The patient needed to feel comfortable enough to give an accurate description of symptoms. The doctor needed to use the skill of "attentive listening" to hear the understated, complex problem. The act of getting to know an individual patient proved invaluable at times.

The Blue Book had alluded to "restlessness" as a possible indicator of early severe infection. With the benefit of growing experience, this statement evolved from one that left me puzzled and skeptical to an important addition to my clinical tool kit.

Similarly, becoming aware of the change in Dave's affect proved crucial. Listening to his recall of the "most painful test" he had ever experienced was the key to integrating the clinical puzzle.

Some people refer to this as a sixth sense, but to me it is truly listening and hearing the clues. The music beneath the words.

22

GUARDIAN ANGEL

A high-backed vinyl chair stood against the wall in the corner of the hospital room, out of sight around the bend from the hall entrance. The seat and backrest were faded yellow, worn smooth from years of hours of diligent waiting. Mary sat silently as I walked in. She was unusually short, her white hair and pale dress rendering her monochromatic as she sat immobile, watching Joe sleep.

A week ago, Joe had come to the office complaining of shortness of breath. This was a new complaint and particularly noteworthy since his job required a moderate amount of physical exertion.

"When did this first occur?" I asked as Joe described his new symptoms.

"It started about three weeks ago," he said. "I have to move some heavy boxes from one room to another as part of my job. It never bothered me to do this until a few weeks ago. I used to move all the boxes without having to rest. But I started getting winded midway through."

"Are you having any other symptoms? Any cough, fever, chills, or pain? And how many pillows are you sleeping on?"

"Well," Joe answered, "I started noticing that my arms felt sore after carrying a few boxes. That never happened before. I didn't have to rest long before continuing. When I started up again, my arms felt OK. It's funny that you ask about how many pillows I'm sleeping on. Around the time this all started I began using a second pillow at night. I'm not sure why – just seemed to be a little more comfortable."

The changes can be so subtle at first; but they begin to fit a pattern.

"Joe, this could be coming from a blockage in an artery supplying your heart. It would be a good idea to do an exercise stress test."

Joe looked thoughtful. "How do you do that?" he asked. "What's involved?"

"He'll do it," Mary interrupted. "Whatever you think, Doc, we trust you."

Joe looked over at his wife. "Yes. Sure."

And so it was decided.

Mary came to the office with Joe when he was scheduled for his treadmill. I promised her that we would let her know when the test was complete. She wanted to be with him when the results of the test were discussed.

The ECG leads that would assess Joe's heart during exercise were connected. Then he began to walk on the treadmill belt. For the first three minutes the belt moved slowly, and the elevation was minimal. He didn't have discomfort or ECG changes. As the belt sped up slightly and the "hill" was increased, his ECG started to develop abnormal changes. Before I could ask if he was having symptoms, he volunteered, "It's getting a little hard for me to breathe. My arms are aching a bit, too. Do you have what you need yet? Can we stop?"

Joe's treadmill was abnormal.

We had him lie down for several minutes after stopping the belt. The initial ECG changes resolved as he continued to rest.

"How's your breathing now, Joe? And your arms?"

"I feel fine, like myself again."

In a few minutes he had changed from his exercise clothes back into his street clothes. Mary joined us in the conference room.

"Joe, your treadmill suggests a blocked artery. We should take some pictures of your heart. The procedure is called a heart catheterization or an angiogram."

Joe thought for a moment and started to speak.

"He'll do it, Doc – won't you, Joe?" Mary interrupted.

Joe looked at his wife. He barely seemed to pause or hesitate. "When do you want to do it, Doc?"

So the angiogram was scheduled.

When I walked toward the cath lab at 7:15 a.m. the next morning to do Joe's angiogram, Mary was in the waiting area outside. Joe was already inside, swallowed into the unknown behind the large automatic doors.

"Come tell me what you find, Doc," Mary had instructed me. "He'll agree with whatever you say he needs."

An hour later, she was there as the still-sedated Joe was wheeled on a gurney from the laboratory back toward his room.

"What did you find?" Mary asked immediately. She almost jumped from her chair in her anxiety to know the results.

Although Joe was awake, he was clearly still feeling the effect of the mild sedation he had received at the beginning of the procedure. I promised again to come by in a couple hours, after I'd reviewed the films and Joe was fully awake, to discuss the results of the angiogram with them.

I returned to Joe's room in the afternoon. He had slept off the sedation. Mary sat in the high-backed vinyl chair, watching him. They looked up at me expectantly.

"It's good that you came to see me when you did," I began. "The angiogram showed a severe blockage of one of your heart's major arteries." As I paused to take a breath, Mary jumped in.

"Can you fix it, Doc?"

"Yes, but let's slow down a bit."

And so I began to explain that of Joe's three major heart arteries, only two were normal. There were several options to restore normal blood flow to the diseased third blood vessel, either surgical bypass of the blockage, or repair by means of the relatively new technique of balloon angioplasty. My brief explanation was punctuated multiple times by Mary's affirmation that I should "do what Joe needs."

Her only other question was, "Can you do it today? Or do we have to wait until tomorrow?" After a short further explanation, the angioplasty was scheduled for the following morning.

Joe was completely agreeable. He kept looking at Mary, nodding in agreement as she affirmed that he wanted to proceed with balloon angioplasty.

When I checked on Joe at 6:30 pm, my last stop before heading home, Mary was still sitting in the faded yellow vinyl chair in the corner.

The next morning, she sat vigil as I worked on Joe's artery in the cath lab.

"How long did you say this would take, Doc?" Mary had asked as the orderly came to take Joe to the lab.

"Probably an hour, more or less. We'll take a picture or two, similar to the ones we took yesterday. These will be our road map to the blocked artery. It also depends how long it takes to set up the equipment and then to get the balloon across the blockage."

"I'll be waiting here," Mary said.

"I know," I said with a smile.

In the lab, Joe moved quietly onto the exam table. He, like Mary, seemed relatively confident and relaxed. The angioplasty proceeded smoothly. The blockage in his artery was close to the artery's origin and before any other major branches. It was a straightforward matter to reach it with the dilating balloon catheter.

"We've positioned the balloon on the blockage, Joe." I told him. "We'll inflate the balloon in just a moment. You may feel some of that chest or arm discomfort like you've been having at home. Let us know if you do and if it gets to be too much. When the balloon is 'up,' it temporarily blocks blood flow to the artery."

With that, I inflated the balloon for the first time. My eyes focused alternately on Joe's ECG and the angioplasty balloon. On the first inflation, the balloon showed the typical wasp-waist narrowing in its midportion. After about fifteen seconds, Joe's ECG began to reflect the absence of blood flow past the area of narrowing.

"It's starting to hurt, Doc," he said.

I waited another few seconds so that in all, the balloon had been "up" for about half a minute, and then drew out the X-ray dye that was used to inflate the balloon.

"How's it doing now?"

Joe hesitated a few moments, then said, "It's getting better now."

I did a small test dye injection. Joe's artery had improved, but significant blockage remained.

"We'll be taking the balloon up again," I alerted him. "Same thing. Let me know how it's doing. We'll probably have to blow the balloon up the same way a few more times to get the artery looking normal." After three similar inflations, Joe's artery did appear near normal. It was an excellent result.

"Your heart artery looks good now, Joe. We're going to get these catheter tubes out and transfer you to the CCU. We'll monitor you overnight. You should be able to go home in the morning, and we'll do a repeat treadmill test in a few days. I'm optimistic that your treadmill will be normal now."

Mary was still sitting outside the lab when I completed the procedure and went out to look for her. I shared with her that Joe had done well, that with a bit of luck his artery would heal as if nothing had ever been wrong.

"Thanks, Doc," she said simply. "We trust you."

That night I checked on Joe before leaving. Mary was sitting in the corner, her dress showing wrinkles, her small form seeming to mold into the high-backed chair that had become her temporary home. She would keep watch over Joe through the night.

23

DIANE: A CAUSE FOR WORRY

Diane was scheduled for routine follow-up when I checked the office schedule early that afternoon. A Hispanic woman in her early thirties, Diane was warm and friendly, with an outgoing personality. I always enjoyed her visits. She had been born with a narrowed aortic valve, and the narrowing progressed as she matured into adulthood.

Two years earlier, the strain on her heart from the narrowing valve had become critical and Diane had surgery to replace the diseased valve. Surgery went well. Her new mechanical valve required chronic treatment with blood thinners to prevent dangerous clots from forming. Managing those drugs was an essential part of her post-op and long-term care.

Today, what I'd thought would be a routine visit became worrisome. When I entered the room, Diane was sitting on the exam table in a hospital gown. As I approached and greeted her, I noted patchy areas of fresh bruising on her face and neck; her wrists also had discoloration. A major side effect of blood thinners was an increased tendency to bleeding and bruising, but the extent of *her* bruising was alarming. I opened her gown in the back and saw additional large areas of purple discoloration. She began to speak even as I asked the obvious question: "Diane, what happened to you?"

"I fell. Tripped over a loose rug and hit my head."

"Did you bruise any other areas?'

"There's some black and blue on my back and one shoulder."

I was silent and began to examine her. It took me a few minutes to process what I saw. The bruises on her back and shoulder covered a large area. It was hard to understand how this much bruising could happen from a single fall. There was a clear disconnect between what Diane was saying, her body language, and what I was seeing. I looked her in the eyes. "When did this happen? Are you OK? Did you get seen in the ER and get X-rays and blood tests?"

"No. I just used ice packs as I'd been told." Diane looked away.

I was now suspicious. Someone was hurting her. From what she had told me in the past, she was living with her boyfriend. Her family was not in Chicago. *This doesn't sound right; something more is wrong.*

Then I asked directly, "Is anyone physically hurting you?"

"I fell," she repeated, looking at the floor.

My concern and skepticism must have been transparent because Diane repeated emphatically: "I *fell*. Really, I'm OK." I finished my exam and ordered a Protime, a blood test to measure the extent of anticoagulation. It is run monthly on patients who are on Coumadin. Georgi came in and drew the blood test. She helped Diane get dressed while I added notes in the chart describing the visit and the findings, sketching the areas of bruising on her face and torso in the chart. I didn't know what to do next; I had not experienced this situation before. After brief hesitation I told Diane, "Call anytime if you need help. I'll give you the name and number of a social worker at the hospital who can help you get to a safe place. Reach out to her today and talk to her. She can help you sort out the situation and look at your options."

Then I emphasized, "You need to stay on your blood thinners to keep your valve working properly. Blood thinners put you at great risk of dangerous bleeding from any trauma, even if it's relatively minor. Pressure and ice packs can help with cuts or small bruises, but not with serious injury from falls, car accidents, or blunt trauma. If this happens again, you *must* go to the ER as soon as possible."

Diane looked away, asking only, "When do I see you

for another follow-up visit?" We agreed on a visit in one month just to make sure healing had taken place. I assured her that she could reach me anytime, either through the office staff or by having me paged if it was after hours. I handed her a card with her next appointment. On the back I had written the name and phone number for the social worker at the hospital.

Over the next few days, I couldn't get Diane's visit out of my mind. The same concerns kept playing again and again. *Was the boyfriend responsible? Had I confronted Diane strongly enough? Should I have been more forceful in insisting on a Social Service appointment? When does one notify the police?* I was at a loss as to how to proceed, and these questions were left unanswered as I was drawn into the busy office schedule. Later that afternoon, I called the social worker at the hospital and gave her Diane's name. I shared my concerns and said I hoped she would be calling.

The next month, Diane came in with new bruising. She continued denying that she was being abused, yet she also confided in me that she was not financially able to leave her boyfriend as she had no job or place to live. Her family was in Puerto Rico, too far away to help her out. She couldn't leave and go out on her own. I tried the Social Services offer again. She resisted. I tried to be encouraging, but realistic. Perhaps she could find a job. Perhaps she was underestimating her own potential. Perhaps she was denying her own safety needs. Most concerning: she was at risk of serious injury, or even death.

"You're young, smart, and very personable. You're bilingual. Possibly you could find clerical work at our hospital. They're always looking for bilingual staff."

Diane was frightened and insecure. I tried to encourage her to take the first step to move out with the help of Social Services. She said she would think about it and left with a follow-up visit scheduled in a month.

I saw her for her regular appointments each of the next three months. Each time, I encouraged her to get the help she needed, to find work and end the relationship. But I felt my attempts to be supportive were falling on deaf ears.

One afternoon, she missed her monthly appointment. Georgi repeatedly tried to reach her by telephone. She sent a note to Diane's home address, requesting that Diane contact the office to reschedule and get her blood drawn. There was no response.

Despite repeated attempts to reach her, Diane was lost to follow up. We contacted the social worker again and asked for her suggestion on how we might find Diane. *Should we involve the police?* Diane needed medical follow-up. If she stopped the Coumadin, her risks for complications, including stroke or a lung clot, were significant.

I was never able to get over the feeling that somehow, I had failed Diane. I could only hope that she had finally picked up the phone and called for help, moved to a shelter for protection and was getting the necessary medical care elsewhere.

It bothers me to this day. We now know that domestic violence is a serious public health problem. Reporting abuse has become more crucial than ever and is mandated in all ERs across the country. Unfortunately, many women are afraid to reach out for help. Their needs for safety cannot be met until they are ready to make that call. Today there's a national domestic violence Hotline (800-799-7223). My regret is it was not in place when Diane needed it.

If this happened today, I would use a cell phone camera to document the bruising and send Diane to the ER for evaluation and X-rays. A call to the ER physician prior to her arrival would alert them to a possible domestic violence case. I would also ask to have a social worker see her in the ER. I recognize now that this was a missed opportunity.

24

GATHERING THE TEAM

Seven o'clock, Saturday night.

Less than half an hour after I got home, my pager beeped. In those days the pager didn't even resemble a cell phone, let alone an iPhone. The earliest ones didn't relay a phone number by voice or digital display. Their chirping call signaled the start of a communication ballet that was remarkably awkward by today's standards. First there was the call to the answering service, and then the call to party that was trying to reach you. This all worked well if you had easy access to a standard phone. But if you were in your car, absent a phone, it presented several dilemmas. First was whether to find a pay phone. Remember those? Then you had to hope you had dimes and quarters to feed the machine. Sometimes it was a challenge just to find one that wasn't in a bar, and to change paper money if your pockets were empty of coins.

There was always the option to hold out until you reached home. Or you could turn around and return to the hospital, betting that this was the prudent response since you were caring for several sick or unstable patients. Whatever option you chose, it was a gamble. On weekends, I sometimes had my kids with me on my trips to the hospital. When the pager beeped and I first called the answering service, I identified myself with a doctor number they had assigned. The kids thought it a great joke to hear me say, "Dr. Kleiman, 777."

The call this Saturday evening was from the Coronary Care Unit (CCU) charge nurse.

"Dr. Kleiman," she began, "Rose is doing it again."

Rose was a gentle, grandmotherly lady in her mid-sixties. She had been widowed years before and had a daughter who worked at the hospital. Her petite size made her appear frail, and her soft-spoken mannerisms enhanced this impression. She had been in the intensive front section of the CCU for two days because she was having repeated episodes of an unstable, potentially life-threatening heart rhythm. These arrhythmias had been present for the better part of the two days since her initial hospitalization.

"What heart rhythm is she in now?" I asked the nurse.

"She's been in and out of ventricular tachycardia.

She's on the maximum dose of IV medication, but the rhythm abnormalities are still breaking through."

Ventricular tachycardia (VT) frequently deteriorates into ventricular fibrillation (VF), a totally chaotic and ineffective rhythm. No blood flows during VF, and death follows in minutes. "How long have the episodes of VT been lasting?" I asked.

"About ten to fifteen seconds. She often starts to lose consciousness but wakes up as soon as normal rhythm returns. So far, we haven't needed to use electric cardioversion to break these episodes."

"Has she had any new symptoms when these episodes of VT occur? Have you observed any seizures during or immediately after the VT?"

"She hasn't had any seizures, but she seems a little sleepy and maybe mildly confused."

Rose's unstable clinical condition was worrisome. Although I had left the hospital only a short time earlier, I decided that I needed to see her and reevaluate her status. Perhaps I would find a new, unexpected clinical problem which was contributing to or even triggering her arrhythmia. In any case, even though I had assessed her earlier in the day, I was uneasy managing her care from afar.

Thirty minutes later I was at her bedside. Although her vital signs were stable when she was in a normal heart rhythm, Rose's skin was cool and pale. She didn't have a fever, and her physical examination was otherwise normal. Although she wasn't on sedative medication, she was intermittently confused. Her cardiac exam offered no new clues despite her recurring rhythm disturbances. Repeat laboratory blood tests were all within normal limits. I was forced to conclude that her cardiac rhythm problem had its origin in the heart itself. There was no identifiable precipitating cause for her persistent instability. The episodes of VT were now coming with greater frequency and lasting longer. She was clearly declining. Unfortunately, we had exhausted all the standard antiarrhythmic medications and had no new medications to treat this serious rhythm problem.

Rose's refractory state left me very worried. I could think of only one other option. I knew a colleague at a nearby Chicago hospital, Dr. Richards, who had been studying heart rhythm abnormalities as an area of focused sub specialization. He and I had attended several cardiology conferences together and shared a collegial professional relationship. I knew he had treated patients with problems like Rose's and would have some experience to draw on. A short while and several phone calls later I made the connection.

"Dr. Richards," I began, "My patient Rose has been hospitalized in the CCU for two days with repeated episodes of VT. We've tried treating her with IV doses of all anti-arrhythmia medications available, but her arrythmia has remained refractory to all our treatments. I've rechecked her physical exam and lab parameters and find no issues that could explain or contribute to her continuing problem."

Dr. Richards listened carefully and then began to speak.

"Let me tell you about some new clinical trial experience we have had on similar patients at my hospital. I've been collaborating with one of our cardiac surgeons using an experimental procedure to address this type of problem. It's complicated, but our results to date have been encouraging.

"The abnormal beats that trigger these episodes of prolonged and repetitive VT seem to originate somewhere in the endocardial lining of the heart's left pumping chamber. To date, we have not been able to localize the abnormal sites precisely. We have, however, found that removing large portions of this lining seems to terminate the repetitive VT. It's open-heart surgery, complex and challenging, but our results have been favorable thus far. We have had a minimum of complications. We could offer this to Rose. I will need to speak to my surgeon. If she agrees, we can talk further to Rose and her family."

My concern for Rose had only grown by the hour. The standard treatments had been ineffective. I did know a bit about the cardiac surgeon Dr. Richards collaborated with but had no firsthand experience, never having needed to refer a patient to her. Now, however, there was nothing left I could offer that had not already been tried—and failed. There seemed little choice. It was obviously unacceptable to passively watch Rose deteriorate. If she continued to have breakthrough episodes of VT, she was in danger of dying.

Dr. Richards paged "his" surgeon but sensed that I was ill at ease. He emphasized that he had previously worked successfully with Dr. Elaine to address similar heart rhythm problems. It being Saturday night, she was at a social event not far from us. Soon, she arrived at the hospital, and the three of us met privately in a small conference room just outside the CCU. Dr. Elaine was dressed for the party she had been attending, and the three of us must have been an incongruous sight, somewhat out of synch with the serious problem we were confronting.

I began to recount Rose's clinical history.

"Rose is a sixty-three-year-old female. She has no prior history of cardiac problems nor, notably, any symptoms that might be attributed to cardiac rhythm disturbances. She began having transient dizzy spells about ten days ago. Eventually we were able to trace these to short, sustained episodes of ventricular tachycardia. Thus far, all the episodes we have documented have lasted no longer than about twenty seconds. All have terminated spontaneously. Continuous IV infusions of arrhythmia-suppressing medications have had no apparent effect. Although she's quite light-headed and dizzy with these episodes, she has never completely lost consciousness, fallen, had a seizure, or fainted."

The cardiac surgeon listened attentively and in turn went to examine Rose herself, focusing on Rose's heart, lungs, and peripheral circulation. Her examination, like ours, did not suggest any structural cardiac abnormalities. We returned to the conference room, and she began to share her experience with me.

"Let me tell you about the patients similar to Rose whom we have treated. At this point, we've had experience with about twenty. Their clinical presentations are remarkably similar. All seem to have an abnormal focus outside of the heart's usual electrical conducting system. This site spontaneously generates electrical impulses that trigger heart contractions. When the rate of these impulses exceeds the heart's baseline rate, normal contractions are suppressed. We have found that by surgically removing large areas of the heart's inner endocardial lining, we remove this ectopic site, even though we cannot locate it precisely."

"Have you had any success locating the offending area more accurately so that smaller areas of lining need to be removed?" I asked.

"So far we haven't been able to do this, but it's an area of active research."

With some intense further discussion, the three of us agreed to offer this surgical option to Rose. While we couldn't predict precisely what her clinical course would be without surgical intervention, we all shared the serious concern that any one episode of VT might last longer and have grave consequences. This could result in disastrous falls, loss of consciousness, or even sudden death. The forty-eight hours that she had spent in the CCU receiving intravenous medications seemed like a reasonable trial period of more "conservative" therapy.

With this decision, I felt at once stressed and burdened, yet hopeful. *I wish medicine were an option for this frail, elderly lady; surgery has lots more risks.*

We located Rose's adult daughter, who was the only family member with her, and went together to update Rose on our concerns and recommendations. She was faced with a somewhat common situation. A patient would be asked to undergo a treatment based on the explanation that their physician offered. But it was impossible to expect the patient to understand the complexities and nuances of the decision they were asked to make. I tried to make the explanation straightforward but honest, describing the risks of this surgery.

I began speaking to Rose, reviewing her clinical course and the various medical treatments we had tried without success. At that point, we paused and introduced her to the cardiac surgeon.

"It seems that you have a spot inside your heart that won't behave the way it's meant to," the surgeon began. "But we do have a surgical approach that can remove it.

We have found in a small but credible number of patients with similar issues for whom this operative approach has been effective. We have done this procedure on twenty patients to date. We have been successful in curing the rhythm problems in seventeen. Although it requires serious open-heart surgery, we have not had any major complications."

"What do you think, Doc?" Rose asked, turning to me.

I had no real experience with the surgery being proposed or with the surgeon who would perform it. All I could really call on was my prior personal relationship with Dr. Richards. I was being asked to put complete faith in his endorsement of "his" cardiac surgical associate. To go forward required a leap of faith on my part. It would require the same of my patient and her daughter: they had to put their faith in *my* experience and clinical judgment.

But the treatments we were using hadn't been effective even after forty-eight hours of intensive IV administration. Time was working against us. Rose's condition was not improving, and each episode of VT was potentially life-threatening. If the duration of this abnormal heart rhythm increased by only a few seconds, a normal, life-sustaining heartbeat would likely not re-emerge. Rose could not safely leave the CCU in her current condition. As best I could judge, it was riskier to delay than to proceed. I retraced my thought process with Rose and tried to be encouraging but realistic.

"All in all, Rose," I concluded, "of the choices available to us, the surgical option seems to offer the best chance for you to recover."

The responsibility I would carry for this decision weighed heavily on me, despite my optimism. Rose looked at me, and then back at her daughter. She hesitated. *Please God, let this be the right decision. There are no easy choices available.*

"So, you think surgery is the best option?' Rose asked again.

By this time, I had silently thought and re-thought, made and re-made, the decision. Each time, I had concluded that the proposed surgical intervention was the best, ultimately the least risky, and so the most reasonable path forward.

"I do, Rose," I said, this time without hesitation.

"When will you do this?" Rose asked the surgeon.

"I don't think we gain anything by waiting," Dr. Elaine replied. "Sooner is better. The risk only goes up with delay. We should do this tonight. While you're being transferred to my hospital, I'll call in my team so that we can move ahead quickly."

Rose nodded. She looked even more frail now, and smaller in contrast to the three of us, who seemed to loom over her. I imagined this moment was intimidating and overwhelming. She hesitated a few more seconds, and then, looking directly at each of the three doctors standing at her bedside, she said, "OK. I guess we'll go ahead."

With the decision made, we shifted gears from discussion to implementation. It was now 9:30 p.m. on Saturday night. Dr. Elaine's party was far behind her. She made several calls, mobilizing her surgical openheart team. Dr. Richards paged and spoke with several of the heart rhythm medical specialists on his team who would work with the surgeons to provide ongoing medical support. The CCU head nurse called to arrange for a monitored ambulance to transfer Rose to Dr. Richards's hospital. Rose would go directly from our CCU to the other hospital's OR.

In about fifteen minutes the ambulance and EMTs arrived. Although we all anticipated that Rose would remain stable while being transferred, the EMTs were trained to use the defibrillator should her rhythm deteriorate.

My stress, since the first page regarding Rose had come, had been continuous and relentless. Now, just minutes after the EMTs wheeled Rose and her gurney into the elevator to begin her ambulance transfer, my mood abruptly changed. In fact, we all seemed to share a similar emotional letdown, as well as anticipation and worry. Rose had been charming and frail, so we all felt heightened concern for her well-being.

Dr. Elaine turned to us as she prepared to leave.

"Thanks," she said. "I'm optimistic that Rose will come through this well. We should be able to start her operation by about midnight. I anticipate it will take three to four hours. I'll let you know as soon as we are finished."

Suddenly, there was nothing more to do but wait, and there was no reason not to do it at home. Shortly before midnight, I received a call that Rose's transfer had gone smoothly. Surgery was about to begin.

I fell asleep.

At 4:30 a.m. the cardiac surgeon called.

"We're finished," she began. "Rose was just transferred to the ICU for routine monitoring. She'll be managed according to the protocol for all postoperative open-heart patients. Most importantly, her cardiac rhythm has been and remains stable thus far. There have been no further episodes of ventricular tachycardia."

I felt responsible for guiding Rose to have the surgery, but there was nothing to suggest that her problem would have resolved spontaneously. We couldn't keep her in the CCU on intravenous medication and oxygen, with the crash cart at her bedside, indefinitely. She certainly would have remained at high risk for sudden death had she gone home.

Rose's postoperative course was uneventful. In six days, she was discharged home in stable condition. There were no further episodes of ventricular tachycardia. She never again required anti-arrhythmia medications.

I saw Rose regularly in the office for the next ten years. Her heart rhythm remained normal throughout. A Christmas card from her daughter arrived yearly, thanking me for my help on that memorable evening.

* * *

Fast-forward thirty-five years. Another of my patients, Darlene, abruptly developed an abnormal heart rhythm with persisting abnormal ventricular extra beats that took control of her heart. The abnormal heartbeats made her highly symptomatic, plaguing her with dizziness, fatigue, and near loss of consciousness. I thought back to the vexing challenge presented by Rose's case. In the years that had passed, however, the treatment of heart rhythm abnormalities had undergone a technical revolution. It had become a discrete subspecialty, Electrophysiology, within the broader specialty of cardiology.

There was no mention of open-heart surgery or stripping of the heart's inner lining for Darlene. Instead, multiple catheters were introduced through the large blood vessels in her groin. These were passed retrograde through the great vessels and across the heart valves into the heart's pumping chambers. Each catheter could measure the electrical impulse originating at the contact point of its tip with the inner heart wall. As the catheters were carefully moved from position to position within the chambers, the sequence of electrical activation was mapped. Any electrical activity that was premature or out of sequence was documented. Once identified, these sites of inappropriately timed impulses were inactivated by careful, very focal, catheter-mediated burning or freezing (ablation). The whole procedure took three hours or less. Darlene was sedated but remained conscious. No cutting or suturing was required, and she was discharged the following morning.

Although Rose lived and was treated in a different time, her similar case was more dramatic, as she didn't have the benefit of more sophisticated and less invasive technology.

It was tremendously gratifying that Christmas cards from Rose's daughter continued to arrive for two decades after that fateful Saturday night.

25

YOU BETTER BE RIGHT

The heart surgeon quickly threw the sterile drapes over the sleeping patient. His staccato motions and accelerating pace belied the veneer of calm he tried to project.

"You better be right or Milt's in big trouble. You'll kill him." he said.

* * *

From time to time, patients with end-stage kidney disease may develop inflammation of the thin connective tissue pericardial sac that surrounds their heart. Fluid frequently accumulates between the heart and the pericardial sac as the result of this inflammation. If the fluid build-up occurs slowly, the sac can stretch to accommodate it. But if fluid accumulates too rapidly, or the volume of fluid becomes too great, this liquid encases the heart. The pericardial sac becomes a stiff container that pushes against the walls of the heart and prevents it from filling. This in turn deceases the volume of blood that the heart can pump to the body.

At first this is gradual, and the effect may be tolerated. But if fluid continues to accumulate or accumulates too rapidly, at some point the pericardium can no longer stretch. A tipping point is reached. Now, adding even a small amount more fluid to the pericardial sac, causes the blood pressure to drop precipitously. Circulatory collapse follows. If the fluid is not drained immediately, the patient's life is at risk. The medical name for this condition is cardiac tamponade.

No two people respond to this condition in the same way. There is wide variability in the rate of fluid buildup and in the stretch that any one person's pericardium allows. The body does its best to accommodate. The heart rate increases to offset the decreasing volume of blood pumped with each beat. But as a person reaches their individual tipping point, disaster becomes imminent, and an unusual physical sign occurs. This is called "paradoxical pulse." Paradoxical pulse refers to a pronounced drop in blood pressure occurring each time the person inhales, only to normalize when the person exhales. To this day, doctors do not fully understand the mechanism of this phenomenon, but it is a reliable clinical sign caused by few other conditions.

* * *

Ed was known among the cardiology fellows for being easygoing and clinically astute. I was pleased to learn that he was the senior attending physician assigned to my rotation on the Stanford cardiology consultation service. One afternoon, Ed was leading our team when an urgent consultation came in. We were asked to determine if a kidney dialysis patient with falling blood pressure was suffering from cardiac tamponade. After the team presented the clinical history, Ed examined the patient at the bedside. Looking for possible evidence of cardiac tamponade, he placed his left hand on the man's chest and watched it rise and fall in time with the man's breathing.

"Up – inhale, down – exhale."

"Feel the pulse," he offered. As Ed's hand rose, the patient's thin, rapid pulse disappeared, only to return as his hand sank when the patient exhaled.

Up, and down; up, and down, I thought. There was a rhythmic beauty to this classic demonstration of paradoxical pulse.

We had already seen the pericardial fluid accumulation around our patient's heart on cardiac ultrasound. Demonstrating paradoxical pulse confirmed that the accumulation had reached the crucial point. Soon thereafter, the patient was on his way to the OR to have the pericardial fluid drained.

* * *

Georgi looked at the list of office appointments. I was running late again. She reviewed the schedule, deciding which patients needed to be seen first, who was sickest, and who needed an ECG or blood test that would appropriately fill the unexpected waiting time. She walked from room to room, chatting with the patients, catching up with news of their lives, noting telltale signs of unexpected problems or needs.

Milt waited quietly in the front examining room. He had been having chest pain. Georgi expected that today he would finally decide to go ahead with an angiogram and consider bypass surgery if it could be done. She had spoken with him in the office and by phone over the past month and noted the increasing severity of his symptoms. She weighed him, took his blood pressure and pulse, and explained that with the office running somewhat behind, Doc would be in shortly. She offered a magazine to shorten the wait, but today Milt was expansive. As Georgi engaged him in light conversation, he began to reminisce about his childhood, and how he had chanced to come to America.

"It was 1905. My family lived in a small village in the Ukraine that had a Jewish community of about twenty families. My father worked as the village miller. It was a difficult time. Anti-Semitism was rife, and there were frequent pogroms." He paused and stared across the room. Slowly he began again, hesitating as he searched his memories.

"It was Friday evening, the Sabbath. The cantor recently had been to St. Petersburg and had returned wearing a pair of splendid new leather boots. As he led the congregation in prayer and song, there was a sudden commotion.

"Three Cossack soldiers, peasant vigilantes, entered through the synagogue door. The leader saw the cantor's new boots. He demanded that the cantor give the boots to him.

"'I won't survive the winter without my boots,' he pleaded. One Cossack drew his saber, and in that instant a slaughter began. The cantor was killed first, and then the fleeing congregants were attacked. My father and I were sitting near the door." The Cossacks had moved past Milt and his father when they first entered. In the chaos as the Cossacks fled, they managed to elude the attackers.

That night, Milt's mother began to bake bread. This was strange because cooking is forbidden on the Sabbath. His parents gathered their few possessions, putting on or packing all the clothes they could. Shortly after nightfall, they loaded the family's clothes and belongings onto a straw-filled wagon. They covered Milt and his little brother, Eddie, with coarse, heavy blankets. It was so cold. Milt could see his breath freeze in the air.

The family set out under the darkened sky. The night's silence was broken only by the breathing of the horses. Milt drifted off to sleep, his little brother by his side. Hours later, when they reached the Polish border, the loaves of bread revealed a secret stash: gold coins, baked into the bread, which were used to bribe the border guards.

Milt recounted the perils of his exodus. His brother Eddie, also a patient of mine, had been only three years old. "For him," Milt explained, "the life he remembers began here in America."

Later, on the day of this recounting, Milt embarked on another journey. He agreed to be scheduled for the angiogram of his heart's arteries. This would soon uncover life-threatening blockages and lead to his coronary bypass surgery.

*　*　*

By 2 p.m. on Friday, Betsy, the surgical nurse, had only a few more things to do before she was finished for the week. I spoke with her briefly on the Cardiac Stepdown Unit. Milt was doing well postoperatively and would be discharged the next day.

"I'm removing his pacemaker wires now," Betsy told me. And then she hurried on her way down the hall.

Cardiac surgical pacemaker wires are lengths of fine wire, about the thickness of sewing thread, that were attached to a needle. With a few quick strokes, four were sewn through the front walls of Milt's heart: two for the upper atrial chambers and two for the ventricles. The wires are then led through the skin. If the heart rate slowed excessively, the wires could immediately be connected to an external pacemaker to keep the heart rate at an acceptable level. They were usually removed three or four days postoperatively. Since these wires are not tied or secured in any fashion, they are simply pulled directly out through the skin. In Milt's case, perhaps Betsy had simply forgotten they were still in place. Milt had had a stormy postoperative course and the wires had probably been overlooked.

It was 3:30 p.m. Milt was restless. Betsy had come by earlier and removed the pacer wires. This had taken less than a minute and involved only an instant of mild discomfort. Now, though, an hour later, Milt felt tired, maybe a trace short of breath. He slept fitfully for a few minutes at a time. His wife, Claire, was in his room and wanted him to go for a walk. She was anxious about his impending discharge to home.

"We need to be sure that you'll be strong enough to make it at home," she said. "Honestly, I'm worried. Do you think you'll be able manage?" she wondered out loud. "You know, I thought you were too old for this operation." After all, she thought, she was almost seventy, and he was eighty-four.

But Milt had been having chest pain for days, and as

it increased in frequency and intensity, he had grown desperate. Then he finally accepted the angiogram to assess the blockages in the arteries in his heart. The results were ominous. All three of Milt's major heart arteries and one large branch were filled with plaque. More than 95 percent blockages were present in all four. Surgery had been suggested; then it had been strongly advocated. Claire had balked and held Milt back. But his pain continued to come, growing insistent, compelling. His medication regime was increased. Claire became irritated with the task of tracking all these medicines. Some once a day; some twice; a few three or four times daily. It was too much, and Milt also quickly grew burdened by the recurring painful and exhausting episodes.

Now he had had the surgery.

Look at him, she thought. *Is he better off?* Again, Claire asked Milt to go for a walk, as if to prove to both of them that he would be strong enough to get himself to the bathroom at home, or down to the kitchen for breakfast. Milt agreed to his wife's request, but quickly returned to bed. He felt light-headed and weak. He lost his breath quickly. Milt needed to sleep; the short walk had left him exhausted. He'd been stronger yesterday. Claire was discouraged.

* * *

Very early in my career, I developed the habit of doing an end-of-the day quick re-check on any patients who were fragile, post-operative or post-procedure, or in the intensive or coronary care units. I affectionately labeled this practice "mop-up rounds." It might consist of only a brief visit in the patient's room to look at a wound or check blood pressure or temperature. Even the exchange of a few social words allowed me to assess the patient's alertness, comfort, or anxiety. This practice was a plus for everyone. The patient felt reassured, and it gave me peace of mind that no unforeseen problems were developing.

Over the years this practice had undoubtedly saved me many adrenalin-filled return trips to the hospital in the middle of the night. Most importantly, though, it had saved many patients the danger of having little problems blossom into full-blown unanticipated crises. This habit had a rhythm to it. I would visit those patients who caused me the most concern first. If any tests needed to be ordered or additional consultations requested, there was more time left to get them done before day's end. Time worked with me as I finished seeing the other patients also on the list before I doubled back to see the most fragile patients one last time.

So, it was not unusual that on this Friday, when I was

through seeing patients in the office and had wrapped up my last dictation, I headed back across the street to the hospital to mop up before going home. Milt had just dozed off when I walked into his room. I was upbeat, glad to see that this fragile, elderly gentleman had made it through bypass surgery and was now on the mend, but his appearance left me unsettled.

"How are you feeling this afternoon?" I asked him. "You seem restless."

"I'm doing OK, but I was really more tired today when I tried to walk than I was yesterday."

"He didn't even walk down the hall as far today as he did yesterday," Claire commented. "I thought he'd be getting stronger by now. How are we going to take him home if he's this weak?"

I looked carefully at Milt. He did appear restless, maybe anxious, yet he claimed he felt well. I tried to probe, unsure if I was overreacting or sensing something real.

Claire complained again about his fatigue and weakness. She was clearly frustrated, and her lack of confidence in him seemed to further undermine his.

I checked Milt's vital signs. His pulse was irregular, as it had been for days, because of his persisting atrial fibrillation. His average rate was about 90. I checked the chart and found that the rate had increased since earlier in the afternoon. His blood pressure was 120/65, also lower than earlier but still a very normal value.

"How do you feel, Milt?" I asked again, almost pleading. "Are you feeling as good as this morning?"

"I'm OK, I'm OK," he said quickly, but without a great deal of conviction.

There were a few more patients to see, and a dozen ECGs that needed reading. I would take one last look at him before leaving for home.

My return visit forty-five minutes later did not assuage my concerns. If anything, it was more disconcerting. Milt's restlessness had become more obvious. He moved to and fro on the bed as we spoke and paused mid-sentence several times to catch his breath. His average heart rate was up to 100 beats per minute, and his blood pressure had fallen by another 15 millimeters.

I ran through a mental checklist of possible issues. Bleeding, new heart attack, and infection topped the list. I ordered a blood count, ECG, and portable chest X-ray. Then I wondered if Milt could be bleeding from removal of the pacemaker wires and decided it would be helpful to get an ultrasound picture of the heart to evaluate that possibility. The technician would be out the door momentarily, given that it was now 4:30 p.m. on a Friday afternoon. A quick call was well timed, and we had her on her way to Milt's bedside within minutes, pushing her big electronic cardiac ultrasound module.

*   *   *

A call to the cardiac surgeon was in order. Although the possible problem and its potential severity were still far from clear, a second set of experienced eyes couldn't hurt. Anyway, I had a couple of patients that I needed to talk to him about.

"I can't talk," Greene said. "I have to finish some paperwork, and then I'm going home."

I insisted that he take a look at Milt before leaving. I was worried.

"Any concern that Milt may have bled from pulling the pacer wires while he's on Coumadin?" I asked.

It wasn't that there was a great alternative. Milt had atrial fibrillation, an irregularity in the rhythm of his upper heart chambers. Stopping the blood thinner carried its own risk that a dangerous clot would form in his quivering atrial chambers. This could potentially cause a stroke or some other serious complication. And a patient certainly could not be discharged with the pacemaker wires dangling from his chest wall.

Greene, with true surgical certitude, was dismissive. "Never happens. I saw him just before I came to the office. He's fine."

Although Greene preferred not to worry, we had worked together far too long for him to be comfortable ignoring my cautionary note.

"I just want to avoid any post-op complications," I

said, knowing this would hook him for sure. I wanted to assure a second, independent re-check.

* * *

Anne had started her medical career almost twenty years earlier as an ECG technician. She had recently learned cardiac ultrasound, generally referred to as "echo." Many times the echo exam provided life-saving, vital information. And for diagnosing pericardial fluid accumulations, the echo was first choice. Anne liked the direct interactions with patients and physicians that emergency studies required. Often, the physician would be at the bedside as they worked together to optimize the study.

Despite Milt's cooperative nature and Anne's considerable facility, the study proved difficult. Milt's anatomy had been distorted by the surgery, and his labored breathing and rapid heart rate made the image quality suboptimal. It was tough to decipher. There was a collection of fluid, but I couldn't be certain if it was directly surrounding the heart, or deeper in the chest near the lungs.

The latter was very common postoperatively, and not a cause for grave concern. Things were also made difficult by the early scarring that was beginning to form after the heart operation. Fluid could accumulate in localized pockets that were difficult to visualize, and where their harmful physiologic effect was disproportionate to their size.

*　*　*

I met Greene in the ICU and reviewed the data with him.

"Milt's blood count is normal except for the usual post-op anemia. White count isn't up, and the differential count is normal. There's no fever, no bleeding in his GI tract. Chest X-ray is clear, the heart size is a bit increased; ECG doesn't show any acute changes. Blood pressure has been falling—it's now 90, and his heart rate is averaging 110 to 120 beats per minute. Neck veins are up, but they have been all along, and this could all be from his chronic lung disease. It's hard to tell with this atrial fib because it's so irregular. And it's hard to tell if his BP changes with breathing at these rates."

I was growing concerned that Milt was bleeding into his pericardium, accumulating bloody fluid that was compressing and strangling his heart. I was becoming convinced this situation was urgent. If I was right, Milt needed to get back to the OR immediately, to drain the fluid off and then assure the bleeding site could be controlled. It wasn't the blood loss alone that threatened him but the liquid leaking into a scarred, confined space, encircling and compressing his heart. I shared my suspicions with Greene, highlighting my growing concern.

"You're asking me to take this guy back to the OR, but you're not sure what's going on. We can get cultures to check for infection, we can give him some more fluid, and we can repeat an ECG in an hour. If you're wrong and we re-operate, he's dead, and it will because of your wrong judgment," he countered in a rising voice. "You can't read his echo, but you're telling me to take him back to the OR to drain fluid that we can't even see!"

When Greene felt threatened, he would often become animated or dismissive. It was hard not to get drawn in by his ad hominem attacks. Yet it was necessary to make the best decision for the patient – and, importantly, Greene was very experienced and had excellent clinical judgment. It was critical to analyze the clinical situation carefully and not respond to his emotional noise.

I tried again to check for a fall in Milt's arm cuff blood pressure with his breathing, looking for the telltale sign of paradoxical pulse. But it was impossible to track his blood pressure with the cuff because of his fast and grossly irregular heart rate. Milt was also breathing harder now, and his blood pressure varying more widely. Greene had suggested that I put a pulmonary artery catheter in his heart and check the pressures. This procedure could have strongly supported the diagnosis of cardiac tamponade but would have taken an hour. Things had deteriorated so quickly that I was sure Milt didn't have this time to spare.

I reached over and held Milt's wrist with my right hand, finding his rapid and thin pulse beneath my first two fingers. Gently, I placed my left palm on his chest.

Dr. Ed, I whispered quietly under my breath, and closed my eyes to concentrate. I clearly recalled the demonstration of paradoxical pulse he had shared years earlier.

Like a kid's seesaw. I tried to shut out everything but the rhythm of Milt's breathing and the varying strength of his pulse. Slowly it became clear that his pulse disappeared when his chest rose with inspiration and returned when he exhaled. I focused, finding the pattern. It was there, discernable, so I became convinced that Milt's clinical deterioration was due to cardiac tamponade.

I needed to speak with Milt and his wife. My concern was apparent even as Milt sensed his own physical discomfort and deterioration.

"Milt, I'm worried that fluid is collecting around your heart. The fluid may be choking your heart and keeping it from pumping effectively. Maybe this started when we had to take out your pacemaker wires a few hours ago. In any case, once we're sure that this is what is going on, Dr. Greene will have to take you back to the operating room to drain this fluid. It's not a big operation, but it's still surgery. We think it's the best way to get you back on your feet as soon as possible. The risk should be very small, and it would be much riskier not to drain it."

Even as this discussion occurred, Milt was sinking. He was now dozing on and off, his breathing becoming more labored. The conversation was really with Claire, and with their son, who had been summoned by Claire as her own anxiety grew.

* * *

Milt slipped into a dreamlike state. It became difficult for him to discern what was happening and what he was dreaming. He struggled to keep the images away. He recalled being bumped, and then again, he saw the synagogue door fly open. The blast of arctic winter air and the Cossack reached the cantor at the same time. Milt recognized the metallic sound of a saber hitting bone. Then there were screams and confusion and people running. The Cossack proudly pulled on the dying cantor's boots and swaggered forward. Milt's father dragged him away from the carnage.

Then his head cleared briefly, and the images were gone. He thought he saw his wife and son walking quickly beside him. He didn't understand their intense look of concern. As he struggled to talk to them, again it was Friday night. Despite the Sabbath interdiction, Milt's mother silently baked bread. Their ghetto home was shuttered. The bouncing wagon sped up. At the border, the hastily baked bread yielded its gold coins. The odyssey west continued.

There were bright lights and the Cossack peered down at him. But the Cossack was talking to him in English, not Russian, and wearing a mask. Then, as hard as he tried, he could not fight off sleep any longer.

* * *

"You better be right," Greene began again. But it was now pro forma. He had accepted my diagnosis of cardiac tamponade, half in trust, half in desperation. The surgical team had assembled quickly, minutes before they were to leave for the weekend. The procedure now was what was colloquially called "crashing" – doing the essential things to get the patient anesthetized, establish a sterile operating field, and begin surgery as quickly as possible. Time was critical.

Milt's ECG and blood pressure were constantly displayed in real time on the monitor. His blood pressure had fallen further and was low now, averaging 60 to 70 millimeters of mercury. This was well below the generally accepted threshold for shock.

Greene was in his element now: focused, operating as quickly as possible, hopeful that he would find what had been predicted. It took him less than two minutes to reopen the original incision from Milt's bypass surgery, done only a week earlier.

I stood just behind Greene on a small step, peering over his shoulder. He quickly exposed the pericardium. "Here we go," he said, and with a quick stroke of the scalpel made a small incision in the glistening pericardial membrane.

A jet of blood shot toward the ceiling. Judging from its height, the pressure choking the heart must have been intense. Stunned, Greene jumped back, and stared for a minute in disbelief. He quickly placed a suction catheter into the cavity to drain the bloody fluid.

I glanced at the monitor. Milt's pressure was back over 100 and rising; his heart rate was already slowing.

Greene looked up. "I never saw anything like that," he said. "I guess you're lucky."

"No, Milt's lucky. It looks like he'll be going home before too long."

26

PATRICK: POWER DYNAMICS

During my years as a consulting cardiologist, many patients were referred to me from a large union whose members were long-distance truck drivers. These patients frequently had cardiovascular problems. Many union members smoked and ate processed food and high-salt diets with lots of fried foods. They did little or no regular exercise. Hypertension, elevated cholesterol, and diabetes were common in this group.

Patrick's referring doctor was a very senior primary care physician whose practice included a large number of union members. The consultation request simply said "chest pain." Pat was admitted to the section of the Coronary Care Unit designated for high-risk patients.

I walked into his room and introduced myself.

"I'm Dr. Kleiman, a heart specialist. Dr. Williams

asked me to see you. What brings you into the hospital today?" I often began my medical history taking in an informal style. I found that this helped put patients at ease and allowed them to feel more relaxed.

"I've been having chest pain when I load heavy boxes into or out of my truck," he began. "The pain usually goes away when I rest. Over the past week or two the pain started coming every day. It's lasting longer now and getting worse. I'm starting to have trouble catching my breath when it comes. I have to stop what I'm doing and rest or the pain lasts or gets worse."

"On a scale of 1 to 10, how bad is the pain you're having?"

"It's an 8 of 10 now most every time it comes."

I continued to take his medical history. Although my tone was conversational, I followed the template learned in my first physical diagnosis course. By the end of this part of Pat's evaluation I had a good idea of the onset, duration, intensity, precipitating activities and nature of his symptoms. I then did a complete physical examination with particular attention to his heart, lungs, abdomen, and blood vessels. Even though the physical findings for a patient like Pat conformed to a predictable pattern, from time to time doing a thorough physical exam led to important unexpected findings.

Pat was in his early fifties. His presentation was classic for anginal chest pain due to blockages in the coronary arteries that supplied blood to his heart muscle. He had several factors that put him at risk for hardening of his arteries: he had smoked for about thirty years; he was moderately hypertensive; and his cholesterol was very elevated. I reviewed his lab and his ECG. Notably, the ECG did not show any evidence of a prior heart attack.

I excused myself and called Dr. Williams, the referring doctor, to update him on the exam.

I reviewed my findings and assessment, sharing my conclusion that Pat needed a coronary angiogram to determine the extent and severity of his arterial blockages. The intensity of his symptoms made it unwise to do an exercise stress test. Dr. Williams agreed.

I came back to Pat and told him that I thought it necessary to take pictures of his coronary arteries to decide how best to proceed. I explained how the angiogram would be performed and scheduled the test as first case the next morning.

As I was bringing him to the cath lab the next morning, Pat told me that he'd had chest pain several times during the night. The presence of rest angina added urgency to his situation. If surgery or angioplasty were necessary, it would be best for him to move ahead with his intervention without delay. His clinical course suggested that he could have a full-blown heart attack at virtually any moment.

His angiogram was uncomplicated, but he had several brief episodes of angina during the procedure.

Given Pat's history his findings were not surprising. He had 85 to 90 percent blockages at or near the beginnings of each of his three major coronary arteries.

Pat needed surgery immediately. I checked with the CV surgeon, Dr. Dave, to see if we could get him on the schedule urgently. Dr. Dave confirmed that he had an opening that afternoon.

I called Dr. Williams again.

"Pat's angio confirmed that he has severe triple-vessel disease. He needs bypass surgery urgently. ASAP! I talked to the CV surgeon, and he has time to do the bypass this afternoon."

To my surprise, Dr. Williams replied, "I'm leaving the hospital at noon, and I don't have time to see or talk to Pat. I'll talk to him tomorrow morning."

"I think it's urgent that he have surgery this afternoon. Given the rest angina he's been having, he could have a big MI at any moment."

"Ask the CV surgeons to put Pat on for tomorrow afternoon. I've got to leave. I'll talk to him in the morning. Then he can have his surgery."

"But Williams, Pat's a classic medical time bomb."

"Tomorrow!" With that, Dr. Williams slammed down the phone.

I moved Pat back to the front of the CCU, where the sickest and most unstable patients were. I put in an order for complete bed rest and that he remain NPO. Then, I called the CV surgeons again and had them reschedule Pat for the following afternoon, leaving enough time for Dr. Williams to see him in the morning before he went to the OR.

I checked on Pat one last time at about 7:00 p.m. before I left the hospital. I had added a couple IV meds to his treatment to help stabilize him, and he seemed to be resting comfortably. I was uneasy but didn't see any other options. I went home hoping for the best.

At about 5:00 a.m. I got a call from the CCU Resident. Pat was having severe chest pain. His ECG now showed changes of an acute MI on the front of his heart. His blood pressure had dropped and was barely holding above shock levels. I rushed to the hospital. The CCU resident had stabilized him so that he was now holding an adequate blood pressure, if on the low end of acceptable.

Pat had a very rocky course over the next few days. His surgery had to be delayed due to his acute heart attack, but he survived and recovered from his MI. He sustained significant damage and was left with a weakened heart, so he was forced to take early retirement. He could no longer handle the physical effort needed to load and offload heavy boxes. Six weeks after his heart attack, he had successful triple bypass surgery.

I found Pat's case particularly disturbing and kept rethinking it. Dr. Williams had pushed aside my best clinical judgment. *I was insulted and angered.*

Dr. Williams's behavior irritated and threatened me.

On the one hand, delaying treatment of a critical, unstable patient was irresponsible. On the other, Dr. Williams was the referring doctor and had a relationship with the patient. It was hard to push back at him, as he had proven himself resistant in the past. He *would* retaliate.

I thought about calling the CV surgeon and sending Pat directly for bypass, but this would also be seen as a challenge to Dr. Williams's authority.

Both situations were risky. I was in a bind. Realizing that Pat was in the CCU and would be closely monitored overnight, I scheduled the surgery for the next afternoon.

Interpersonal dynamics between physicians are difficult to manage at times. The most important lesson for me was to trust my clinical judgment and experience and insist that patients get timely care.

Dr. Williams and I parted ways a few months later. The conflict had become too intense. I was no longer able to tolerate having my clinical judgment ignored and patients put at risk. Pat recovered and was able to get a good surgical result, but his life was forever changed.

In Pat's case, I had followed unwritten hospital rules. As the referring physician, Dr. Williams was further up the chain of command. As the consultant, my hands were tied. In the best of all possible worlds, hospital politics would not impact clinical patient care. In this case, they did.

At this time in the eighties, primary physicians controlled the referral of patients to the specialist. This reality was imperfect and continues to be challenging. It is my view that the patient's needs should always be at the center of care.

Conflict is present in the workplace, and decisions often must be made in real time. Clinical judgment plays an important role in team decisions. Unfortunately, not all doctors are team players. All opinions carry weight and are pertinent to these decisions and outcomes. Sometimes differences present a dilemma in treatment plans. Standing firm on your best judgment is important, but at times it can be difficult.

27

A NEAR MISS

The head nurse pushed the exam room door halfway open. Leaning in, she said, "The EMT's just radioed. They're bringing in a young kid. They say he's bleeding badly – he's got a deep cut in his arm." There was urgency in her voice.

"Put a hold on four units of O negative blood," I said. "And get an IV set-up ready with normal saline. We should be ready to go when he gets here."

"Did you get any more information on the boy they're bringing in?" I asked a few minutes later, adding, almost in the same breath, "Page the surgeon on call. Let him know that we may need him."

Before the nurse could answer or get to a phone, we both heard the wail of a siren, growing louder as it approached, and we turned toward the large ER doors. As they opened, the ambulance pulled up, its tires screeching. The EMTs quickly transferred the patient and gurney through the doors and into the Trauma treatment room.

"Vital signs: BP 95/65. HR 120, and he's bleeding heavily from a deep cut under his right arm," the EMT barked. "Transit time, ten minutes. We got a 20-gauge IV with saline in his left arm. We tried but couldn't get in a second larger IV. The kid's name is Mike."

I turned back to the nurse. "Keep trying to get that second IV in. Use a large one, an 18-gauge if you can. Draw a CBC, lytes, clotting parameters, and check that the blood bank types and cross-matches him for a total of four units of blood."

The new patient was a young boy who appeared to be in his early teens. I walked quickly to his side. "What's your name?"

"I'm Mike; I'm thirteen," he answered in a faltering voice. "It was my brother Hal. He didn't mean to. I don't want him to get in trouble."

Mike was lying on his back. The right side of his shirt was soaked with blood from his shoulder to his waist. His right arm was slightly raised and rested on three or four green surgical towels. They had been stuffed up into his armpit, filling the space between his arm and chest wall.

I did a quick exam. Mike's BP had fallen to 90 systolic and his heart rate climbed to 130 beats/minute. His lungs were clear, heart sounds normal, and abdomen soft. His skin was cool, pale, and slightly damp.

I turned to the nurse. "Get me some more surgical towels," I said. "I'm going to unpack this and take a look at his laceration."

I put on a pair of surgical gloves and carefully began to peel away the layers of wet, bloody towels. As I lifted off the one directly on top of his wound, blood spurted out with some force. The bleeding was heavy, making it impossible to see exactly where the cut was in his artery. I quickly grabbed two dry towels and repacked the space under his arm, applying pressure as I did. I turned back to the nurse. "How's the second IV coming?" I asked. "Any luck?"

"His veins are collapsed, Doc," she answered. "I can't find any good veins."

"I can hardly stay awake," Mike said softly. "My mom should be here soon," he added in a fading voice. There were small beads of sweat on his forehead.

The EMT standing by Mike's side turned toward me.

"He lost a lot of blood on the way in. Soaked through two green towels before we got him packed with the ones that were under his arm when he got here. The site is too far in to get a tourniquet around it. We could get his vital signs on the way here, but his blood pressure was faint."

Another nurse came over to see if any more help was

needed. Together we transferred Mike from the ambulance stretcher to the hospital gurney.

"Mike, how are you doing now?" I asked. "You lost a lot of blood. We're going to get you patched up."

Mike was awake and coherent but subdued. He seemed to fade in and out of consciousness. I gave a few more orders to the second nurse.

"We really need that second IV. Keep trying to start it. Have we sent the STAT blood work yet? Get a blood count, clotting parameters, type, and crossmatch for four units of blood. Also get a background metabolic profile."

Despite the nurse's continuing efforts, it became clear that Mike's low blood pressure and heavy blood loss were making it impossible to find a suitable vein to start an IV. He was in impending shock. The nurses were having trouble even drawing blood, let alone starting an IV. The one the EMTs had started in the ambulance was small in caliber and running slowly. We badly needed a larger line to get fluid in faster and to transfuse blood as soon as it became available.

"Keep trying," I repeated. "He's lost a lot of blood. I'm sure his volume is low. Get a cut down set to the bedside now." Finally, after persistent efforts, a second, small IV was started.

I turned my attention back to Mike. His skin was now cooler, and still damp; his pulse was thready and rapid. He was fidgeting and restless.

Moments earlier a woman had walked in, following the EMT's as they hurried into the ER. She appeared distressed as she rushed to catch up to the boy. The ER secretary, sensing the urgency, also walked to the exam room to get the information needed to register Mike.

"Are you Mike's mother?" I asked, turning for a minute to the woman who had just come in. "Why don't you go with these two ladies," I said gesturing toward the charge nurse and secretary. "You can fill them in while we get Mike stabilized. We'll come and get you when he's set."

The two ladies went into the small ER conference room. The charge nurse turned toward Mike's mother, rapid firing a series of questions. "We need his full name and birthdate. And can you fill us in on what happened? Is he allergic to anything, antibiotics in particular, or is he taking any medications?"

"I'm Marian Green, Mike's mother," the woman began. "He's thirteen."

"Mike said something about his younger brother. He was named Hal," the nurse told her. "Mike said he didn't want to get Hal in trouble. I didn't get a clear picture of what went on between the two of them."

Mrs. Green started to fill in the details of what had happened.

Her two sons, eleven and thirteen, were playing together as she began to make dinner. The boys seemed to be on autopilot, and she hadn't been paying much attention to them. At one point they filled a couple of squirt guns and started trying to spray each other – things started to get wild before she realized it. The younger of the two, Hal, had been hiding. Apparently, he surprised his older brother Mike with the squirt gun. Hal started running, and Mike chased him. Hal ran out the front storm door, which had a glass upper panel. Without giving it much thought, Hal paused and pushed the glass door closed. This put it straight across his brother's path.

By now, Mike was running after his brother at full speed. He extended his arm in an attempt to catch the door before it closed. In the excitement of the moment, Mike's extended arm and hand missed the door handle and hit the glass window with full force. The glass shattered, and Mike's outstretched arm was caught on its jagged edge. Both boys froze. The screams that followed brought their mother rushing. A steady stream of blood was running from under Mike's arm toward his waist. Hal, though stunned and shocked, had the presence of mind to put pressure on the bleeding site and managed to slow the bleeding a bit. His mother dialed 911.

In the ambulance, the EMTs packed the wound with towels. They said they'd slowed the bleeding a little but couldn't stop it. Blood kept running from under Mike's arm and armpit.

"Wait here," Sheila, the charge nurse said.

I turned to Sheila as she came back into the ER

trauma room. With growing concern, I asked, "Did you reach the surgeon on call before? If not, page him again. Keep on trying until you reach him." The urgency in my voice reflected my increasing worry. The hemorrhage needed to be stopped; Mike had already lost a significant amount of blood. It needed to be replaced as quickly as possible.

Time continued to work against us.

"We haven't been able to reach the surgeon," the nurse said. "We've tried several times to contact him without success."

"Are there any surgeons at all signed into the hospital? There must at least be one," I said with a mix of hope and fear.

"Doc," the nurse said, "do you know what day it is?"

"Of course," I answered, annoyed. "It's Friday. So what?"

"Doc, it's 4 p.m. on the Friday before Memorial Day weekend. People are checking out mentally, if not in person."

Meanwhile, the IVs started before by the EMTs, and again in the ER, were too small to allow blood, which would likely soon become available, to be transfused. They were of modest help, since they did permit some clear fluid to be infused, but Mike's blood loss had made him low on volume. His condition was somewhat akin to severe dehydration. His veins were partially collapsed like unfilled pipes.

The nurse looked up. Her worry and frustration were apparent. "I'm having trouble getting another a large line started," she said. "Can you help?"

Mrs. Green walked to the doorway of the ER conference room. She had overheard part of the conversation.

"Is he going to be alright?" she asked. "He doesn't look good. I'm worried."

Trying to reassure her as much as possible under the circumstances, I said, "We're trying very hard to reach a surgeon to fix Mike's artery. And we'll keep trying until we reach someone."

I turned back to the nurse and said quietly, "Help Mrs. Green back to the waiting room. Reassure her that we'll keep her updated on Mike. We'll let her know if there's any change in his condition."

But Mrs. Green had reason to worry. Mike would deteriorate seriously if we weren't able to start to transfuse him and replace his blood loss. With her question, the gravity of the boy's condition began to weigh more heavily on me. Up till then, I had been treating Mike by reflex. I had examined the wound in detail earlier, hoping to locate and isolate the lacerated artery. Then, even if we needed a surgeon to repair it definitively, at least we could apply pressure directly to control the bleeding until the repair could be done. But the cut in Mike's artery was deep inside his axilla (armpit). He was bleeding too fast for us to see in detail what was going on; his artery was in a pool of blood, and we couldn't keep the wound dry long enough to identify the cut in it clearly. In theory, I could put a hemostat or other pliers-like surgical tool deep into the axilla and clamp a large bundle of tissue without identifying the artery.

But that approach was risky. The artery in the axilla is very large. It is the major branch supplying blood to the whole arm and hand and begins very close to the aorta itself. If I damaged this artery, a major, more complex vascular repair – possibly requiring insertion of a graft –would be necessary. There could easily be permanent severe damage and Mike could end up needing an amputation. There is also a large bundle of nerves that runs through the axilla alongside the axillary artery. Blindly clamping these nerves in the jaws of a surgical tool could severely damage them, leading to disabling loss of function even if his arm were preserved.

I turned back to Mike. The pressure the nurse was able to exert deep into his axilla had slowed his bleeding some. It was at least to the point where, if we had a large IV, we might be able to start to make up his blood and fluid volume loss. Hopefully this would be sufficient to stabilize him, buy us time while we continued to reach out to find a surgeon.

I paused to consider our options. There were several possible ways to get the access to a major vein that would allow us to rapidly infuse the volumes of blood and saline Mike desperately needed. The routine approach, using his arm veins, was insufficient. One possibility was to insert the type of large-caliber sheath used to perform heart catheterizations. Inserting one of these into his large femoral vein would be a good solution. This vein is present in everyone; its location is constant at the junction of the upper thigh with the pelvis. I turned back to Sheila.

"Do we have any 7 or 8 French size sheaths, the kind used for catheterizations and angiograms?" I asked.

"Doc, we don't do those procedures in the ER. We don't stock them. I have no idea where Radiology keeps the ones they use."

This was really a setback. Using one of these sheaths, which I had a great deal of experience inserting, had seemed like a good solution. Even if there were some stocked in the X-ray department, we had no idea where to begin to look and looking would waste valuable time.

Another possibility was to start a large size IV in the vein that coursed under Mike's collarbone. Alternatively, there was large vein, the internal jugular vein, which ran from the neck into the upper chest. While either of these veins was a possible target for a large IV, he was low on blood volume, making it technically difficult to enter them. Either of these approaches could be complicated by unintentionally nicking the upper tip of his lung, which could cause the lung to collapse. Given Mike's fragile state, such a complication would be very dangerous.

I decided to fall back on a different approach. I knew I could do an accepted, though not routine, procedure. In medical school I had done several operations on anesthetized dogs to learn basic surgical skills. One was a "cut-down," which speaks to its direct surgical approach. Often used as a means of giving medications or fluids, this is a method for surgically isolating a vein that lies just beneath the skin, traveling next to the ankle. To access it, a small cut is made in the skin covering the vein; then, using the rounded, narrow tip of a hemostat for blunt dissection, the vein is isolated from the surrounding tissue. A small incision is made into the exposed wall of the vein. Under direct visualization, a large caliber IV infusion tube is introduced through the cut in the vein wall and passed directly into the lumen of the exposed vein. It was a means of delivering large volumes of fluids and medications. Today, Mike would benefit from this past training.

There were several benefits to doing a cut-down on Mike. The vein used was at a site far from the traumatized axilla area and would allow me to insert the large caliber connector directly into the vein itself. We could then "pour" large volumes of fluid or blood directly into the boy's vein. In this case, we had cross-matched blood for him waiting to be transfused; doing a cut-down on the vein on the side of his ankle would allow us access to transfuse the blood rapidly and safely. It seemed the perfect solution.

I turned back to Sheila. . As I turned, I saw the blood bank technician arrive with four units; she quickly verified that it was the correct blood for Mike's blood type.

Although I had not recently performed a cut-down, my memory of the procedure was accurate and clear. In less than five minutes the vein was isolated. The large end of the infusion set was readily secured inside Mike's ankle vein. While the nurses continued to apply pressure up and inside the axilla, slowing the rate of hemorrhage, we began rapidly infusing the first of several units of blood. When those finished, Mike received another liter of saline IV fluid as well. His blood pressure and alertness responded favorably. While we had not done the "definitive" axillary artery repair, between the partial control of his blood loss and the ample blood and fluid infusions we had started to stabilize the situation.

I said to myself, *This kid is going to survive.*

There had been a time when I feared Mike might bleed to death or, at best, suffer severe injury to his right arm. But we now could keep up with his blood loss and buy some time.

I walked back to the waiting room. Mrs. Green was nervously pacing. I had barely walked in when she asked urgently, "Is he going to make it? Will he be OK?"

"We got a big IV in. He's getting blood transfused right now. We just spoke to a surgeon. He'll be here in a few minutes. Mike is going to be OK."

Just then the surgeon came through the doors and headed into the ER. Dr. Ross quickly focused his attention, carefully removing the surgical towels that were still pushed up against the inside of Mike's axilla. He turned to Sheila.

"We'll need a vascular repair kit and a Gore-Tex patch," he said. Then he looked at the cut-down site on Mike's ankle where blood was still rapidly infusing.

"You did that?" he asked, turning to me. "Back to the basics!"

"I learned it in medical school. We operated on dogs and learned to keep them alive," I answered with relief.

"I expect you'll make a full recovery," Dr. Ross said with a smile, addressing both Mike and Mrs. Green. He was able to isolate the artery and control the bleeding. The cut in Mike's artery was large enough that it needed to be patched and could not be closed directly. It took Ross almost an hour to finish its repair. When he finished, he checked Mike's pulses at his wrist and foot. They were both strong. Mike's skin color was returning to its normal pink.

Mike's overnight stay in the ICU was uneventful, and he went home a day later. His arm recovered full function.

To this day the possibility of losing Mike from hemorrhage had worried me more than any other case that I did or would encounter.

When the surgeon arrived and took control of

Mike's care, I felt a tremendous sense of relief. I had a son very close to Mike's age. He, too, was full of mischief, and it was easy to imagine him in a similar predicament. Focusing intensely on Mike helped push aside those parental emotions.

Although I had never been confronted with a patient having an acute, life-threatening hemorrhage, I had prior experience with the clinical skills needed to manage this crisis. These included finding and controlling the bleeding site and establishing vascular access for blood and volume replacement. Fortunately, these individual skills came together when needed. More importantly, a few years later it became the standard of care that for an ER to be designated a Trauma Center and receive trauma patients, a surgeon had to be on-site and available 24/7.

BACK TO BASICS

My wife and I were on vacation and enjoying dinner at a cross-country ski lodge when we met Ed. Ed was about sixty years old and worked for the federal government as an officer in the Treasury Department. Although his job was primarily sedentary, from time to time he would do some household chores. He loved to play golf in warmer weather and enjoyed cross-country skiing in Montana during the winter months.

Over dinner, Ed learned that I was a cardiologist.

"Do you treat aneurysms?"

"Well, generally, yes," I replied. "What type of aneurysm?"

He looked puzzled.

"An aneurysm is a swelling or ballooning of a vessel, usually an artery. As a person ages, aneurysms can be caused by a tear in a vessel wall, elevated pressure within the vessel, or hardening of the arteries. Aneurysms may occur in many places, though there are several more common locations."

Ed looked at me intently. His focus tuned out the other guests and their conversations. "Can I tell you what happened to me?" he asked. "I'd be interested in what you think."

Conversations like this were not uncommon at social gatherings. I enjoyed and valued them. They often provided important insights into how people came to medical attention. Sometimes, they highlighted organizational challenges that made it difficult for patients to access the care they needed. The conversations felt engaging, and rarely intrusive.

"About ten months ago, I started having backaches," he began. "I spend most of my workday sitting at a desk. But from time to time, I do some reasonably heavy lifting when I'm working around the house. In the past I've had occasional mild backaches, but this time they were more intense and persistent. At first, I got some relief from Advil, but then the pain started breaking through."

Ed's story did not sound particularly unusual, and I listened without comment as he continued.

"After a few weeks like this, it seemed that the pain was beginning to get worse."

"Did your pain ever wake you at night or keep you from sleeping?" I asked. Assessing pain's effect on a patient's sleep pattern was a metric that I often used to roughly gauge its intensity.

"It did, and although I'd strained my back once or twice before, this time it seemed worse. One of my friends suggested that I see his chiropractor, and in desperation I decided to see if he could offer me some relief. I made an appointment as soon as I could, and so saw him in his office a couple of days later." He paused and looked at me. "What do you think?"

I smiled. I knew what I would have been sure to do before deciding on my next clinical step. "Well, there's a long list of conditions that can cause back pain, ranging from muscle strain to spine-disc issues, to ulcers, to abdominal aneurysms. These days a patient would probably be sent for a CT scan or other imaging. That would, in fact, be appropriate," I said. "Notably, all these amazing imaging tools, like CT scanning, MRI, and two-dimensional ultrasound, have been developed and become widely available only in the past thirty-five years or so.

"For sure I would have started by carefully examining you to give me some clues as to the best way forward. Did the chiropractor examine your back and belly?"

"He did," Ed answered. "And when he did, he clearly

was surprised. He said he could feel something pulsing in my abdomen that was the size of a small apple. He said it was probably an aneurysm and was large enough to be in danger of rupturing. He arranged a CT scan that afternoon, and it did show a large aneurysm. I had surgery one day after that."

"Smart chiropractor. When abdominal aneurysms get to be about two and a half or three inches in diameter, they have a major risk of rupturing. Doing a surgical repair before rupture is critical and is much safer than delay. It was crucial that the chiropractor examined you. Feeling the aneurysm pointed him in the right direction so you didn't lose valuable time. The expanding aneurysm was pushing against your back and spine. Your pain was a warning sign. I'd keep his phone number in your contact list," I said.

The impact of the chiropractor's skillful diagnosis most likely saved Ed's life. Patients who sustain the rupture of an abdominal aortic aneurysm have a mortality of greater than 90 percent. Ed was spared this catastrophic event because his chiropractor did a careful physical examination. He had him lie down and felt his belly before addressing his back pain.

Ed continued to ski for another ten years, only stopping as his advancing age became limiting. My wife and I also continued to vacation during that same week, and so were able to witness Ed's survival over the years. By chance, Ed lived in a Chicago suburb, as we did, and this conversation led to a long-term friendship.

Ed is still alive many years after our chance meeting on the slopes. His longevity bears witness to the wisdom I first heard spoken by Dr. Bill in his wonderful gravelly voice many years ago: "The first thing I would do would be to take a thorough medical history and perform a detailed physical examination." Ed's chiropractor did this and saved his life.

* * *

Two men stood outside the patient's room. Both doctors, one senior and one junior.

"It's classic, but uncommon. See if you can find the clue."

The junior doctor went into the room and spoke to young man lying in bed. The patient looked fit; nothing was obvious.

"How long have you had hypertension?'

"Only recently that I know of."

"How did you find out? What was bothering you?"

"A life insurance exam. Nothing was bothering me. The doctor found it when he examined me. He said my exam was unusual and that it all pointed to a coarctation of the aorta."

The junior doctor was surprised. "What suggested that diagnosis to him?"

"My pulses and blood pressure. He said hypertension was not common at my age. Told me a medical adage, 'Hoofbeats usually mean horses, not zebras.' But I was a zebra.

"The pulses in both my arms felt strong, but weak in both my legs. He trusted his own exam and checked arm and leg blood pressures using a blood pressure cuff. Confirmed the differences. Said there had to be a narrowing in the aorta."

"Do you understand now what's going on?" the younger doctor asked.

"Not really."

"Coarctation of the aorta is a defect generally present at birth. It is a narrowing, often severe, of the aorta, the main highway carrying blood to all parts of the body. Usually, the defect is an inch or so long, just past the affected area, the aorta returns to its normal diameter."

The patient looked confused.

"OK, so there's a narrowing, but why the difference between arms and legs?"

"The aorta comes out of the heart and travels upward. It gives off branches to the head and arms and then curves downward. Think of it as starting out heading north and then making a U-turn, going south. The narrowed part lies after the origin of the branches to the head and arms. This makes the blood pressure lower in the legs than in the arms."

"What do you do about it? Will it go away?"

"It almost always needs surgery, never goes away by itself. Once there's a clue like your blood pressure differences, imaging – like a CT scan or an angiogram – confirms the diagnosis. That was one smart doc checking you out for insurance. He did a good physical exam and trusted it. I'd like to examine you now. I will be repeating much of what the insurance doctor did. Then I can discuss treatment options with you and answer any other questions that you have."

When the junior doctor repeated the physical exam, he was able to demonstrate the wide difference between the arm and leg blood pressures. "I get the same findings on my exam as the insurance doctor did. I'll schedule a CT scan."

"What's involved in the surgery?" the patient asked.

"The surgeon will find the area of narrowing in the aorta. Once he's located it, he may remove it and reconnect the aorta using a Gore-Tex tube. Sometimes the surgeon can widen the aorta with a Gore-Tex patch and doesn't have to remove the narrowed area. Both approaches result in making the aorta functionally normal again. I'll talk to your attending physician and see how soon we can get your operation scheduled."

Two days later the patient had surgery.

Cardiac diagnoses can be made by healthcare providers other than physicians. On occasion, these providers find meaningful clues to a patient's underlying problem. The two preceding stories illustrate situations in which critical findings on physical exam were made by non-physicians. Fundamental to each of these findings was a hands-on bedside examination. Then, high-tech testing confirmed the initial clinical impression. New technologies build upon the basics, but they are an adjunct, not a replacement. High-tech can never replace high touch, and artificial intelligence can never replace the human brain.

29

MEMORIES

ALL THINGS IN MODERATION

Sister was a cheerful nun in her early sixties, barely five feet tall. She was soft-spoken and reserved. Like so many people in their middle years or older, she had developed high blood pressure. This had been documented on several occasions on routine office visits. In the past, Sister had been reluctant to start antihypertensive medications and wanted to try following a low-salt diet.

"Doctor, I really don't want to be taking pills. Can you let me try again to see if we can get the pressure down? I'll really try hard to avoid salty foods. This time I think we can do it." Sister was earnest in her appeal. She looked straight at me and repeated her request. It was difficult not to be moved by her sincerity.

"Sister, let me have the nurse give you some printed handouts that may help. They review the types of foods that are high in salt. You may be including some of these in your regular diet and be unaware that they're the offenders. For example, canned soups or canned tomato products usually are very high in salt. So are lunch meats – salt is commonly added to enhance their flavor. Let's try dietary salt restriction one more time and see if we can make it work. You'll really have to be careful."

"OK, doctor," Sister answered. "I'll really try."

"I'll get you scheduled for a follow-up visit in six weeks. That should be long enough for us to see if we can make it work." With that, I put instructions on Sister's chart to give her the literature on low salt diet and review it with her and to schedule her next office visit.

Six weeks passed, and Sister once again came to the office for a blood pressure check. I walked into the exam room where she waited patiently.

"How's the diet been working out?" I asked.

"It's gone well," she answered. "I've really been trying."

"Well, let's check your blood pressure and see how we're doing," I answered. I was hopeful that this time we'd turn a corner for the better. I put the blood pressure cuff on Sister's arm, inflated it, and carefully watched the needle as the air was slowly let out. Her blood pressure was still quite high at 170/95 mm. Discouraged, I inflated the cuff again and repeated the measurement.

Still high. Way too high.

"Diet doesn't seem to be working, Sister. Are you sure that there aren't times when you go off your diet? Any lapses?" I asked as I looked directly at her.

The nun's affect changed. She looked at me, then at the floor, and then at me again.

"Well, occasionally I slip up. Like I did last night. We had a party. It was Sister Louise's birthday. I couldn't miss the party. I love it when we party." She looked at me with a shy smile.

I was speechless. I thought nuns were a serious group. I had no idea whatsoever that they partied. Incongruous images flashed through my mind: nuns having a beer, dancing on the tables, and keeping the beat.

"Well, Sister," I asked, "How do you and the other nuns party? What do you do when you party?"

Sister looked away again and then, reluctantly, met my eye.

"We eat pizza," she answered.

Before Sister left, we agreed after some discussion that getting on a medication was in order. I gave her samples for a two-week trial and a follow up visit with Georgi, for a blood pressure check.

Everyone needs to party now and then.

GREETINGS

One of the most rewarding and beneficial aspects of following patients over time is the relationships that can develop. In addition to helping, you learn the pattern of medical issues affecting the patient, social interaction becomes warm and friendly. This makes for enjoyable and satisfying appointments that can feel like visits with a friend. On occasion, the openness and familiarity that develop may provide clues when problems arise.

Bernie was such a patient. He was about fifty-five years old, heavyset, a military veteran, and predictably cheerful. He loved to garden, and often shared tips and seeds with Georgi. On one visit, he brought in heirloom green bean seeds for her garden.

Our visits always began the same way.

"How are you feeling today, Bernie?" I'd ask.

Raising his hands, turning his palms up and looking directly at them, he would reply, "With my fingers, Doc."

Curtis also had a signature opening that never varied. A fifty-five-year-old Black police officer, he was soft-spoken, impeccably dressed, and slightly formal. He had high blood pressure and family history of heart disease. His visit was always in late afternoon, after he finished his shift, and he arrived in his full uniform. He was a high-ranking police officer, used to being in charge and giving orders, and seemed uncomfortable and out of his element in a healthcare setting. He was also a Black man entering a white medical world on the north side of Chicago. The way he took control and relieved stress was with gentle humor.

Meeting him as a person and not as a patient helped to make the process more relaxed, and allowed me to get more information on his health status. When I walked into the examining room, Curtis was waiting for me with a broad smile. As I prepared to greet him, he invariably beat me to it.

"How are you feeling today, Doc?"

"Doing OK, Curtis. Thanks. How about you?"

Another smile would follow.

SAM

Sam was an eighty-eight-year-old retired attorney, stately in bearing with a gentle, kindly affect. He lived right near the office and came in once a month for evaluation of his heart failure. He was always accompanied by his wife and a caregiver. Sam was having some mild memory changes, so having his support people there made the visit more effective. His office visits always began with the same dialogue. "Doc, I want to be sure to remember not to forget to remember what I wanted to be sure to remember to ask you today," he'd say earnestly.

"Don't worry, Sam. Let's think this through together. Try writing your questions down before you come in next time," I'd answer.

I asked Sam and his wife a few short questions to get an idea of how things were going at home.

How is your weight doing? Are you seeing any weight gain?

Are you having any shortness of breath at night?

Still sleeping on two pillows?

His wife would generally answer for him.

"Let's go over your medicines and make sure you're getting help in taking them daily and on time. Georgi will write them down on a card for you to give to your caregiver. Most important is, you must stay on your low salt diet. We'll remind your caregiver of that too.

"Please help Sam continue to take and record his BP twice a day," I said to his wife. "Weigh him each morning before breakfast, and call if you see a jump of two or three pounds overnight. Sam, on your next visit, have your questions written down when you come in – that way you don't have to worry that you'll forget something important."

Memory loss is a common problem with older patients. With cardiac patients, it can exacerbate management. Working with family and caregivers may be necessary to achieve compliance with diet and medications – the more they understand the nature of the problem, the better they're able to support the patient and call when needed. Striking a balance between recognizing a memory problem and treating a seasoned professional with caring and respect is essential to management.

THE GUY DOWN THE STREET

Bob was a regular who came into the office three or four times a year. His wife Kathy always joined him. Bob was a Korean War vet. A large man, he was energetic, somewhat informal, and always friendly. He had originally been sent to me for management of a leaky heart valve. Although his physical examination showed characteristic features of his diagnosis, his findings and symptoms suggested that the leak was small, or moderate at most. A heart ultrasound exam confirmed this assessment.

Bob had very recently retired and now filled many of his days playing golf, which he loved. One of his office visits was punctuated by an interaction that was initially quite puzzling. I had just told him that it sounded like his leak was stable and hadn't increased. He lost his usual jovial affect and looked at me earnestly.

"Doc," he began. "You gotta take care of me. I'm starting to worry about Buck."

His comment left me confused. In the three years he

had been my patient I had never once heard him mention a person named "Buck."

I asked the obvious question. "Who's Buck?"

Without a doubt Bob's answer was of a sort I had never heard before and would never hear again.

"Doc, I'm worried about Buck," he repeated. "You've got to keep me alive. I haven't met Buck yet, but I know he's out there waiting. Two of my best friends died in the first six months after they retired. You can't let that happen to me. If I die, Buck will be trying to move in with Kathy, drive my new sports car, and he's going to be playing golf with my new set of clubs. Doc, I mean it, you gotta take care of me." Then he repeated, as if for emphasis, "No. I don't want Buck moving in."

It took me a few seconds to get past my surprise. I put my hand on his shoulder and moved a bit closer. "I understand," I said, looking straight at him. "I've got you covered; I've got your back."

DRESSING FOR THE OCCASION

As Georgi came out of the examining room, she had difficulty keeping a straight face. It was difficult for me to imagine what could be so amusing about helping an elderly lady change into a medical gown and prepare for her examination.

Trying not to laugh, she said simply, "Wait until you see Edith. She's in a gown now and ready for you."

I was in the dark. Edith was a new patient – sort of. She was eighty years old. I had been caring for her longtime boyfriend, Marty, for many years, and Edith had accompanied him on nearly all his visits. Although the nurses and I recognized her and knew her by name, she had never previously been seen as a patient.

She recently had been told that she had hypertension and was bothered by sporadic palpitations. When she first came into the office that day, we had exchanged a few words before Georgi took her to an exam room. I recognized her at once but thought it perhaps a bit unusual that she was dressed up as though was on her way to an evening party. She wore a dress that was notably fancy for a visit to a doctor's office. Her hair was set very stylishly and dyed the red color that I guessed she'd had in her younger days. She wore a pearl necklace and high heels, again more suited to an evening engagement than an afternoon doctor's visit.

I greeted her briefly. "Hello, Edith," I began – but she interrupted and spoke coyly, a lilt to her voice.

"Hello Dr. Kleiman," she said. "I figured after all these years I've been bringing Marty to see you; I should get myself in with a handsome young doctor who will be here when I start to get old."

I was surprised by her tone. I said, "I'll see you in a few minutes, Edith."

Given Edith's manner and the unusual exchange

with my nurse, I wasn't sure what to expect. I asked Georgi to be in the room while I examined her.

The only thing that I could think of that was a bit unusual about Edith, but certainly not terribly funny, was that she was overdressed. She had obviously also fortified the coloring of her red hair to keep it as close as possible to what it must have been in her youth – it had a strong orange tint.

The nurse and I sat down in the exam room with Edith. I proceeded to take her medical history in detail, given that this was her initial patient visit. "I'm going to examine you now, Edith," I then said in my usual fashion, having nearly completely forgotten the earlier exchange with Georgi. Edith loosened her gown and I reached to place my stethoscope on her chest.

And then, the cause of Georgi's earlier surprise became clear. In marked contrast to her colorful red hair and very white complexion, Edith wore black, lacy undergarments, complete with a black garter belt.

For a few moments I was speechless. Then, struggling to regain some degree of composure, I completed her exam.

After the initial visit I continued to see Edith every three months. She was followed with periodic echocardiograms. Her valve function remained stable, and she never needed open heart surgery. Her initial presentation was never repeated, nor was her choice of undergarments.

A LASTING MEMORY

Sid was a tall attorney in his late sixties who carried himself with a cheerful, yet stately, bearing. A very senior cardiologist, now retired, initially referred him to me. Sid came into the office regularly for treatment of his ongoing atrial fibrillation.

As I walked into the exam room on this afternoon, I noted that Sid and I were dressed quite similarly. Sid was wearing a solid blue sport jacket, dark khaki slacks, and a light blue oxford shirt with a button-down collar. But it was his tie that caught my eye. His tie was made of dark yellow silk that blended easily with the khaki color of his slacks and embellished with small geometric figures in a blue tone that was nearly the same as his solid blue sport jacket. This minor coincidence captured my attention because I had recently purchased a similar blue blazer sport coat and khaki slacks outfit.

"Good morning, Sid," I began. "Have you been feeling any uncomfortable palpitations since we started you on the new medicine?"

"No, Doc. The medication we started on my last visit seems to have done the trick. My breathing is much less difficult. I've rarely, if ever, felt bothersome palpitations since we made the change."

"I'm very glad to hear that. Sounds like we should hold steady with this regime. Hopefully, it'll continue to work well. I'm going to do an ECG to document your progress. Let's plan to see you again in three months. Call in the interim if you have any problems."

Sid and I chatted a bit more. Then I turned to him and said casually "Sid, I notice we're both dressed alike today. Your yellow tie seems to be a perfect match to bring the slacks and blazer together. Do you remember where you got it?"

Sid looked at me and didn't say a word. He loosened his tie, took it off, and placed it around my neck.

"It's yours, Doc," he said.

I was embarrassed and surprised. I protested. And protested. "I didn't want to take your tie," I repeated several times.

Sid countered each time, saying, "It's yours. Doc. I want you to have it."

In the end, all I could say was thank you and accept this unanticipated gift graciously. I still wear Sid's tie with my blue blazer more than thirty years later.

BON APPETIT

George was about eighty-five. He, like so many others who are part of the great diversity that makes America, had immigrated to the United States in his early teens to escape persecution. Like so many others, his story was also one of hard work, determination, and ultimate success on both the personal and financial levels. Like so many in his age bracket, he also had moderate hypertension, a modest elevation of his fasting blood sugar, and high blood cholesterol and triglyceride levels. He was the father of one of my dearest friends. His office visits always felt like family visits, as his son and I had shared many sailing adventures together over the years.

George happened to have an office visit shortly before lunchtime one day. His blood pressure was again elevated in spite of a regime of two powerful antihypertensive medications. His routine blood tests again documented high blood cholesterol and triglyceride levels in spite of prescribed statins. He also had an elevation of his fasting blood sugar.

Much of the office visit was spent reviewing with George the need to bring these metabolic and hypertensive abnormalities under control. But it was not a new song; it had been played before.

Our conversation was not new. "George, I'm worried about you. We want to keep you going until you're 100, but you have to cooperate. Following the right diet will really help get some of these values into normal range. The better the numbers, the better your chances. I'm going to ask our nurse-dietician to go over things again with you. We've got to work together to make this happen. It's important."

"Thanks, Doc," George replied. "This time I'm really going to try," he said earnestly.

A few minutes later I saw our nurse go into the room where George was waiting. Then, as I finished seeing my last patient of the morning, George left, carrying several pages of supplemental reading materials firmly in hand.

I went back to my desk and finished some paperwork, and then left the office and walked across the street to the hospital. My stomach reminded me that it was lunchtime, so I decided to go directly to the cafeteria before beginning my rounds. As I walked with my tray, George sat with his back toward me, eating at a table nearby.

What a great time to see George beginning his new diet, I thought, and walked over just in time to see him vigorously deploying the saltshaker as his partly finished lunch plate came into view. It became clear that a plate of fried chicken had been the target of the shaker seconds before. A piece of pie sat expectantly to one side of the main lunch plate.

High salt, high fat, and high sugar, I thought. *Three out of three!* The printed dietary instructions we had given George lay neatly on the corner of the table. As I observed this, he looked up at me, a sheepish grin on his face. I looked at George, then at his lunch tray, then back at George. I rolled my eyes, but before I could say anything, George proclaimed, "But Doc, I thought all hospital food was healthy!"

It's important to know when to retreat, I thought.

"*Bon Appetit,* George," I said as I gave him a friendly tap on his shoulder. "*Bon Appetit.*"

George proved me wrong. He did in fact live to celebrate his hundredth birthday.

30

BROTHER FRED

Brother Fred was unique among my patients. He was a monk who clearly lived what he preached. He considered his mission to live simply, in poverty, and to minister to the struggling and homeless. This generally consisted of helping homeless people secure food and shelter available through local charities or contributions from Brother's followers. As one might expect, this meant that Brother frequently had to sleep without shelter and go hungry. However little he had, Brother always shared with those he saw as more in need. His commitment to his calling was consistently reflected in his selflessness.

A tall, thin man, in his early fifties, Brother was quiet and soft-spoken with a gentle manner. During his office visits he wore a long brown hooded robe that hung loosely, skirt-like, to a few inches from the floor. The robe was tied at his waist with a heavy white rope. The robe's edges were frayed. There were several areas where seams suggested that tears in its cloth had been sewn back together. He wore sandals on his bare feet and these too appeared worn and "tired."

It was never clear how Brother first learned about and came to my practice. He was aware that he had significant high blood pressure and had occasionally sought medical care in a free clinic. He also knew that on more than one of these visits he had been given the diagnosis of hypertension. He had been advised to get ongoing care and follow-up, but his poverty and the unpredictability of his life made compliance difficult.

Brother had never been hospitalized nor had any major illnesses or surgeries. On his physical exam he had a soft heart murmur suggestive of a mild valve leak, most likely in his mitral valve. His routine laboratory test results reflected normal kidney function—specifically, the absence of kidney damage secondary to uncontrolled hypertension. I arranged for him to have an echocardiogram that confirmed the presence of a mild mitral valve leakage. Because Brother was on Public Aid and appointments were difficult to get approved and scheduled, the echo technician did the test as a favor to me.

At the conclusion of Brother's first office visit I urged him to take blood pressure medications on a regular basis. I explained that if left untreated for long periods of time, he would be at higher risk of suffering complications affecting his kidneys, heart, or brain. As I began this discussion it became clear that he had typically seen different physicians at each visit to the free clinic. The implications of untreated high blood pressure had not been made completely clear to him. I told Brother that we would be glad to see him regularly, and that taking medicine daily was very important. Then I started to write him prescriptions, but he stopped me.

"Doctor," he said with some embarrassment "there is no way I can afford to purchase these."

Now it was my turn to be embarrassed. I silently scolded myself for being insensitive. I should have anticipated that compliance would be difficult for him. Of course, I wanted to assure that he would receive optimal medical care. Brother deserved the same care that he gave to his "flock."

"Brother," I said apologetically. "I should have realized that; I have a solution."

At that time, sales reps from the drug companies would provide medication samples to doctors' offices. These starter samples allowed a patient to take a new medication, typically for a week or two, and to be sure it was tolerated before purchasing a full supply of what was often an expensive new medication. This assured the patient that they would not experience serious side effects or allergic reactions to the new drug and have to discard a month's supply. It often made it possible for the doctor to provide sample medications to someone who was otherwise unable to afford them.

It was fortunate for both Brother and me that I had adequate samples to get him started on his new treatment. I could give him enough so he could take it for a meaningful trial period. This would let me know if it was effective and well tolerated.

"Try taking one of these each morning," I said to Brother. "Let's see if this gets your blood pressure under control. If it's working well for you, I think I can continue to get enough samples to keep you supplied." Brother Fred's blood pressure did come under control. We were able to continue to get enough medication samples to keep him adequately supplied to keep his blood pressure controlled.

Over time, Georgi and I were able to donate warm winter clothing, blankets, and boots to Brother. We had many other small items as well as "odds and ends" that he could either use or resell. Soap and washcloths, as well as toothbrushes and toothpaste were highly valued. When Brother was able, he would borrow a friend's car and we would arrange to meet him in the city. Together we would move tires and boxed clothing from our trunk to his, and he would take them to the shelter where he was staying.

From time to time, Brother would miss an appointment. When we would see him again our concern for his safety would ease. The harsh nature of his life and desperate needs of his "flock" contrasted dramatically with our world. Through his extraordinary efforts the benefit of our relatively small gifts was multiplied.

Brother's valve leak did not progress to an extent that required surgery. He continued his good works for many years with kindness and compassion. He gave me a small window into a world that had been totally unfamiliar to me. Fortunately, his health remained strong for a number of years in spite of the medical and physical risks to which he was continuously exposed. I felt privileged to have been able to contribute in small ways to the success of his mission.

Over time, it became apparent that despite the differences in our lives and goals, there were also some clear similarities between Brother's religious calling and the purpose in my medical practice.

Medicine was and remains a spiritual calling or vocation for me, as Brother's service of the poor was for him. Underlying my efforts as a doctor was the goal of restoring health, of healing, or preventing disease. It is this direction and purpose that makes medicine a vocation, an activity with a spiritual direction. In Brother's case, his vocation had parallel goals. The healing he attempted to bring was not only through providing material necessities; he sought to restore spiritual health as well to the unfortunate. He was guided by the desire to protect and care for those in need, and did so with a singularity of purpose. In caring for them, he helped them feel cared for.

In my medical practice and in Brother's ministry, each of us was the giver of service and felt spiritual satisfaction in seeing the results of our efforts. In the end, Brother and I enlarged our world views through acts of service to each other.

In Brother's case, he saw a physician strive to bring healing with efforts that were as committed as those that he brought to his community each day.

Though on the surface my world and Brother's world were quite different, in the end we shared common values and a spiritual commitment that guided us. The gifts of caring, commitment, and compassion were expressed by each of us in our own way. All of them came from the heart.

EPILOGUE

I took early retirement because of medical problems that limited my ability to continue as an interventional cardiologist. I missed the patients that had been essential to my medical practice for over thirty-five years.

Retirement gave me time to reflect on the journey I had made in becoming and practicing as a physician. Patient stories were fresh in my mind and flowed freely. At first, each story seemed to stand alone, but over time, common themes became apparent.

Over the course of my career, revolutionary advances in technology had occurred, and the impact on patient care was dramatic. It was logical to pause and ask myself what had changed, and what was still true and enduring. *What was the essence of doctoring? What had I learned over thirty-five years about the role of* the human connection in the practice of medicine? What was the relevance of these stories today? Could my sharing them serve a new generation of medical students and young doctors? My purpose evolved over the three years of writing. The stories became a tool for sharing the importance of human relationships in medical practice.

The patient stories speak to the need to get to know each patient. Each recounts diagnosis, treatment, and the return of the person to their optimal state of health.

This occurred in several ways; most obvious was learning how the person's current medical situation had taken him from a state of wellness to a state of illness. Recognizing each patient as an individual began the process of understanding the circumstances that affected that person's life. While technology was a tool, and often a very valuable one, it was important for me to remain completely aware that I was always treating a person, not a case – always a *person*, never "a stroke," or "a heart attack," or "a pneumonia."

Disease could have a different presentation in each person. The process of getting to know a patient included discovering their social and family histories. This information provided context for understanding who the person was, and created the basis for a relationship that would evolve and deepen over time. The strength of this relationship was based on many factors: attentive listening, mutual respect, communications, reliability, and trust. My patients and I worked together as partners.

These stories describe the foundation of the physician-patient relationship in a variety of circumstances. I believe they illustrate the satisfaction that both the patient and I experienced when our partnership grew.

* * *

The Covid-19 pandemic began years into my retirement. Isolation, in hospital terms, had a whole new meaning. Pandemic isolation highlighted the pain and loneliness that occur when human connection is compromised. No visitors were allowed in the hospital; nurses and doctors were covered from head to toe in protective gear. Patients spent hours in isolated rooms without the comfort of human contact. Soothing touch was impossible at times; gloves and protective gear denied even this most essential of human needs. Family members were separated from each other, with communication happening by FaceTime or Zoom. With masks on all staff members, communication was impaired. Life-saving machines, while essential for care, left people feeling traumatized. The absence of human contact and direct, person-to-person interaction left healthcare workers drained and emotionally depleted. A huge volume of critically ill patients stressed the system and the doctors, nurses, and ancillary personnel. Some staff caught Covid, and many frontline nurses and doctors were unable to work; thousands died. For those remaining on the job, stress was a daily event. Burnout became common.

These stories took place before the pandemic. They do, however, provide examples of the importance of human contact and connection between doctors and patients, and of their sustaining power.

Now that I am a patient, I am a recipient of care. A recent experience with a well-known specialist highlighted the importance of humanity and mutual respect in healthcare delivery. I had waited for over a month to get an appointment. The doctor walked into the semi-dark patient exam room where I sat and first looked at the computer to see prior test results. He approached me with no introduction and proceeded to examine me with no explanation or conversation, only brisk instructions as needed. When he finished, he turned to me and said only, "It's normal." I tried to ask some questions to help me understand how the test he had just completed impacted my medical problem. The famous doctor cut me off in mid-sentence and repeated, "It's normal! You need to see another specialist." With that, he turned and left.

This doctor may have been world famous, and his assessment was likely accurate. But I did not feel cared for. No relationship was initiated. As a patient, I did not experience any sense of satisfaction.

Seventy years later I still remember how I felt after the in-home visit by my pediatrician for a sore throat. I felt cared for and valued.

My gift in telling these stories is to help foster an approach to your professional identity as a medical doctor. Much of this is now being taught in the "Doctoring" courses offered in your university and many others. Your journey has just begun, and the evolution of you as a practicing doctor is a process that will happen over time.

My *hope* is that your generation of physicians hone the skills so central to rendering care in a compassionate way.

As we return to post-pandemic care, we must recognize – and remember – that the human component of medicine and doctoring remains essential to healing.

ACKNOWLEDGMENTS

I would like to thank the many people who were teachers, mentors, and colleagues and who made this book possible. William Lands, PhD at the University of Michigan and Bernard Moss, MD, PhD at the National Institutes of Health (NIH) first introduced me to basic laboratory biochemistry research. Richard Popp, MD, Robert Goldman, MD, Edwin Alderman, MD, Sharon Hunt, MD and William Hancock, MD were prominent clinical teachers during my cardiovascular fellowship at Stanford University, as was the famous cardiac and heart transplant surgeon, Norman Shumway, MD. Andreas Grüntzig, MD invented the balloon coronary angioplasty catheter and personally taught its use to aspiring cardiologists. He taught small live demonstration courses, one of which I had the privilege of attending in Zurich, Switzerland. Geoffrey Hartzler personally shared his gift in manipulating these balloon catheters and inspired their application in cases of marked complexity. John B. Simpson, MD, a fellow colleague and one time co-worker applied his engineering genius to develop new minimally invasive therapeutic cardiac devices.

Saint Joseph Hospital, Chicago, supported me in the creation of the Angioplasty Institute. The staff who worked with me in the Cath Lab, notably Jonas Juska and Ruth Burgess, were invaluable team members.

A number of friends and colleagues helped this book come into being with their encouragement and feedback. Margo Weinstein introduced me to the process of finding an editor.

Michael Attas MDiv, MD, and Joseph (Jody) Stern MD, both published authors, helped me to understand possible pathways involved in the publication process. Their insights were critical in my beginning to negotiate this complicated path. Additionally, their thoughtful comments and feedback further allowed me to shape and refine the manuscript.

Readers who also provided particularly insightful commentary were Nina Adams, MSN, Nurse Practitioner, Marian Barrell, Mary Avalon Zelasco, Lawrence Frankel MBA, Pam Frankel MS. They were early, and very thoughtful, readers. Moreson Kaplan, MD, Yale Health Plan Administrator, Roger Rueff, PhD, and David Walton, PhD contributed at all stages of the writing. Their thoughts and comments are deeply appreciated. Christopher Wagner, who has retired and has multiple degrees, would rather be sighted as a "careful reader, intellectual sparring partner and close friend since time spent together at Harvard Kennedy School of Government."

Darrin Blumfield provided legal counsel as we moved ahead into the publishing process.

My primary editor, Irene Connelly, was truly an editor extraordinaire! Her availability, and constant encouragement along with her constructive questioning, assured the integrity of the manuscript. She also made sure that the format, language, and flow of the manuscript were coherent and technically correct. Angela Lauria, PhD, of Difference Press, took on a first-time author and acquainted me with the publishing process. Her assignment of Madeline Kosten, editor-in-chief and her team of graphic designers, line editors, and proofreaders have all proved to be invaluable.

A special "thank you" goes to my wife, Georgianna E. Kleiman, RN, BSN. Her diverse background in critical care nursing, Emergency Department medical care and ED practice administration, as well as her years as my practice manager, made her essential in all aspects of patient care. As I began writing this book, I realized that with her nursing experience and perspective, our patients got the best from both us and were assured of receiving comprehensive, compassionate care. Georgi was also my first reader and editor. Without her, this book would never have come to completion. She researched, studied, and prodded me to continue when I had "writer's block" and the task ahead appeared overwhelming and daunting. I could not have had a better partner in this endeavor. Georgi, you have been my muse!

ABOUT THE AUTHOR

Jay H. Kleiman, MD, is a retired interventional cardiologist with over thirty-five years of clinical, biomedical research, and management experience. He was a premedical and medical student at the University of Michigan and medical intern at the University of Chicago. He fulfilled his military service obligation as a research associate at the National Institutes of Health (NIH). He was an Internal Medicine resident at Georgetown University and a subspeciality Cardiology Fellow at Stanford University.

More than twenty years later, Dr. Kleiman's love of clinical research led him to serve as medical director for large cardiac drug development clinical trials. One trial led to the successful introduction of a new medication.

Dr. Kleiman is board certified in Internal Medicine and Cardiology. He is a fellow of the American College of Physicians (FACP) and American College of Cardiology (FACC).

He earned a master's degree in Public Administration (MPA) from Harvard's Kennedy School of Government. He has been an active advocate for patients and physicians over his career.

As a practicing clinical cardiologist at a large university affiliated community teaching hospital, Dr Kleiman was among the first to introduce the ground-breaking technique of cardiac and leg balloon angioplasty and stenting in Chicago.

Dr. Kleiman lives in Chicago with his wife, Georgi, a retired critical care nurse.

THANK YOU

Thank you for taking the time to read *Art of the Heart* and to appreciate the stories within. Reflecting on my career in medicine, I hoped to share some experiences with you that I thought would enrich your training.

As I wrote the stories, I discovered that my connection with patients took place on several levels. While there were clinical lessons in each case to be learned, equally, if not more important was the creation of an atmosphere for interactions conducive to open communication. Please consider and share the ideas central to the concept of partnership that are the basis for a therapeutic doctor-patient relationship.

To reach me for questions or comments, or to receive a free eBook copy with full-color images, email:

Heartfeltpress@gmail.com